In this book Mark Neufeld argues that the predominance of the positivist approach to the study of international politics has meant that theory committed to human emancipation remains poorly developed. He suggests that International Relations theory must move in a non-positivist direction, and takes recent developments in the discipline (including Gramscian, postmodernist, feminist and normative approaches) as evidence that such a shift is already under way. In a comprehensive treatment, he argues that the critical theory of the Frankfurt School can be used to reorient the study of world politics. Drawing on recent work in social and political theory, as well as International Relations, this book offers an accessible analysis of recent developments in the study of international politics.

D1065863

Tom Green

CAMBRIDGE STUDIES IN INTERNATIONAL RELATIONS

Series list continues after index

The restructuring of International Relations theory

Mark A. Neufeld

Department of Political Studies
Trent University
Peterborough, Ontario

CAMBRIDGE
UNIVERSITY PRESS

Published by the Press Syndicate of the University of Cambridge
The Pitt Building, Trumpington Street, Cambridge CB2 1RP
40 West 20th Street, New York, NY 10011–4211, USA
10 Stamford Road, Oakleigh, Melbourne 3166, Australia

First published 1995

Printed in Great Britain at the University Press, Cambridge

A catalogue record for this book is available from the British Library

Library of Congress cataloguing in publication data
Neufeld, Mark A.
The restructuring of International Relations theory / Mark A. Neufeld.
    p.   cm. – (Cambridge studies in international relations: 43)
Includes bibliographical references and index.
ISBN 0 521 47394 2 (hard) – 0 521 47936 3 (pbk.)
1. International relations – Philosophy.
I. Title.   II. Series.
JX1391.N477   1995
327.1'01–dc20   95–7672   CIP

ISBN 0 521 47394 2 hardback
ISBN 0 521 47936 3 paperback

C E

For my mother, Elsie Louise Neufeld,
and in memory of my father, Alfred Harry Neufeld,
with love and gratitude

Contents

Acknowledgments

The image of the monkish scholar working productively in isolation has, for good or for ill, never applied in my case. In the absence of interaction with others of similar interest, I have found creative thinking to be virtually impossible. Accordingly, I wish to acknowledge the many people who read all or parts of this book and provided me with helpful comments and/or stimulating discussion along the way. Among them: John Sigler, Michael Dolan, Rianne Mahon, Tariq Ahsan, Andreas Pickel, Roger Epp, Alex Wendt, V. Spike Peterson, Nicholas Onuf, and, last but certainly not least, Stephen McDowell. To them I owe my thanks.

I would also like to thank my exceedingly able research assistant, Sheryl Shore, for going over the manuscript with a fine-toothed comb, as well as Departmental secretary, Shirley Lynch, for handling my messages and chasing down missing faxes with such good humour and efficiency.

I am indebted to Richard Little and Steve Smith of the Cambridge Series Editorial Board. Without their support for this project, it is doubtful that it would ever have seen the light of day. I benefited as well from the constructive criticisms of two anonymous reviewers. At all times the advice and guidance from John Haslam of Cambridge University Press was much appreciated.

I want to thank my one-time fellow graduate student, Sandra Whitworth. In addition to being the perfect office-mate (she rarely came to campus), she was instrumental in convincing me that a theory of world politics which aspires to be truly critical must be feminist as well.

Above all I wish to thank Tracy Heffernan for her support and patience. Her contribution to this work was both direct (reading and rereading the entire manuscript) as well as indirect (at critical moments, shouldering an asymmetrical amount of child-care so that I could have the 'fifteen more minutes' I needed to 'finish up this section'). Throughout the writing process she helped me keep this project in perspective by reminding me that critical theory also has to have something to say about how I lead my life away from the computer. Above all, she never let me forget that if theorizing is itself a form of practice necessary for emancipatory struggle, it is, nonetheless, a form of practice that can never suffice on its own.

Funding for much of the research and writing of this book was provided by the Social Sciences and Humanities Research Council of Canada.

Selections from chapters 1 and 5 appear in 'The Pedagogical is Political: The 'Why', the 'What', and the 'How' in the Teaching of World Politics', in Lev S. Gonick and Edward Weisband, eds., *Teaching World Politics: Contending Pedagogies for a New World Order* (Boulder: Westview Press, 1992).

An earlier version of chapter 3 appeared as 'Reflexivity and International Relations Theory', in *Millennium: Journal of International Studies*, 22, No. 1 (1993), 53–76; reprinted in Claire Turenne Sjolander and Wayne S. Cox, eds., *Beyond Positivism: Critical Reflections on International Relations* (Boulder: Lynne Rienner Press, 1994).

An earlier version of chapter 4 appeared as 'Interpretation and the Science of International Relations', *Review of International Studies*, 19, No. 1 (1993), 39–61.

Introduction

International politics being but a specific instance of a general political theory, the main task is to understand the requirements and problems of such a theory. For if this assumption is correct, the key to a theory of international politics will not be found in the specific subject matter of international politics but in the requirements and problems of a general political theory.

Hans J. Morgenthau[1]

Maybe there are periods when one can get along without theory, but at present its deficiency denigrates people and renders them helpless against violence. The fact that theory may evaporate into a hollow and bloodless idealism or sink into a tiresome and empty rehashing of phrases, does not mean that these forms are its true forms. (As far as tedium and banality are concerned, philosophy more than finds its equal in the so-called investigation of facts.) In any case, today the whole historical dynamic has placed philosophy at the centre of social actuality, and social actuality at the centre of philosophy.

Max Horkheimer[2]

This book is concerned with providing an answer to a very specific question: why is it that theory oriented toward human emancipation remains poorly developed within the discipline of International Relations? The answer offered is one rooted in an analysis and critique of the predominant approach to the study of world politics – that of positivism. It is argued that it is the internal logic of positivism – the positivist 'logic of investigation' – that accounts for International Relations theory's lack of emancipatory content. Consequently, International Relations theory needs to be 'restructured' in a non-positivist direction; it must be reconstituted as a form of 'critical' theory if it is

1

to make a meaningful contribution to human emancipation. Finally, it is argued that the beginnings of such a meta-theoretical 'restructuring' process are already visible in contemporary theorizing about world politics.

This, in a nutshell, is the central argument being offered. The argument itself will, no doubt, prove sufficiently controversial. What may prove nearly as unsettling, however, is the orientation of the book as a whole. For this is an exercise in international meta-theory. As the notion of 'international meta-theory' may be unfamiliar to the target audience of this work – International Relations scholars – it is important to be clear about the meaning of the term and, by extension, the significance of this type of exercise.

Perhaps the best way to clarify the meaning of meta-theory is by way of analogy. Consider, for instance, the discipline's treatment of empirical evidence. While International Relations is concerned with incorporating facts into explanatory accounts, it has generally not subscribed to what some have labelled the position of 'barefoot empiricism'. That is to say, International Relations scholars have generally not succumbed to the empiricist temptation of assuming that 'facts speak for themselves'. On the contrary, it is generally held to be the case that facts require interpretation in order to have meaning – interpretation which is the product of the application of theory to facts. In short, the meaning of facts is not a factual question, but a theoretical one. Consequently, given that explanation is one's goal, 'there is nothing so practical as a good theory'.

The insufficiency of this widely held position is that it leaves unanswered a very important question: 'what constitutes good theory?' And just as answering the question 'what do these facts mean?' requires a move to a higher level of abstraction than that of the empirical – namely, the theoretical – so also does the question 'what constitutes good theory?'. In short, just as the meaning of facts is not a factual question, but a theoretical one, so the nature of good theory is not a theoretical question but a *meta*-theoretical one.

International meta-theory, then, seeks an answer to the question: 'what constitutes good theory with regard to world politics?' As such, it is a vital part of the quest for explanatory accounts of the subject matter of the discipline. Indeed, if it is true that facts are dependent upon theory for their meaning, and that theory, in turn, is dependent on meta-theoretical reflection to ensure its adequacy, then the general assessment of the place of meta-theory may be in need of significant revision. Meta-theory is not a diversion from the 'real substance' of the discipline, theoretically informed analysis of empirical evidence. Rather, meta-theory is the indispensable foundation of competent scholarly activity and the basis of the adequacy of the explanatory accounts which are developed. Consequently, it can be argued that the relative neglect of meta-theoretical questions in the discipline of International Relations accounts for a good many of the serious limitations to which contemporary theorizing about world politics is presently subject.

As an exercise in international meta-theory, this book must, virtually by definition, attempt to straddle the line between two distinct subfields of social science: 'social and political theory' and 'International Relations theory'. In so doing, it seeks to apply the insights generated within the field of social and political theory to theorizing about world politics.

Of course, this straddling effort is itself rather atypical of a discipline which has for a good part of its existence understood itself to be, in some sense, *sui generis*. In fact, it is becoming increasingly clear that the claim that 'International Relations is a discrete area of action and discourse, separate from social and political theory',[3] can no longer be sustained. It can no longer be sustained because today International Relations is confronted with theoretical challenges it seems incapable of meeting on its own. These include:

(i)   calls for ways to promote meaningful discussion and debate in a discipline increasingly marked by paradigmatic pluralism;

(ii)   calls for theory which is as competent and comfortable in theorizing change in the world order as it is in analysing continuity;

(iii)   calls for theory to guide practice which can address normative concerns as well as questions of practical efficacy.

Grappling with these kinds of issues is at the very core of the field of social and political theory. Hence the insights afforded by social and political theory are now more relevant than ever for the discipline of International Relations.

With these introductory remarks in place, this chapter has four specific objectives remaining: (i) to clarify the research strategy that is adopted; (ii) to draw attention to the nature of the methodology employed; (iii) to note briefly the politico-philosophical specificity of

3

the approach adopted; and (iv) to sketch a general outline of the book as a whole.

Research Strategy

As was noted above, the research strategy adopted is that of applying the insights of social and political theory to the discipline of International Relations. This strategy – and, indeed, a good part of the argument being advanced here – is rooted in Richard Bernstein's path-breaking study of the mid-1970s: *The Restructuring of Social and Political Theory.*[4] Drawing on the efforts of philosophers of science, phenomenologists and hermeneuticists, as well as theorists associated with the Frankfurt School, Bernstein argued that the social sciences were undergoing a 'dialectical movement' of restructuring at a (meta-)theoretical level. The restructuring process posited by Bernstein involved a shift away from a positivist approach to the study of the social world to one which – while not neglecting empirical analysis – incorporates (i) a concern with achieving an interpretive understanding of the intersubjective meanings which constitute that world, as well as (ii) an interest in criticizing that world as part of the effort to change it in a way consistent with the goal of human emancipation.

Bernstein's discussion of a (meta-)theoretical restructuring process taking social science in a critically interpretive, post-positivist direction led me to wonder if his thesis might not also have relevance for the discipline of International Relations. As I began to explore this possibility, I became convinced of three things: first, that a restructuring of International Relations theory in a non-positivist direction is necessary; secondly, that evidence for a restructuring process similar to that outlined by Bernstein already exists in contemporary theorizing about international politics;[5] and thirdly, that the outcome of that restructuring process will have profound consequences both in terms of the discipline's ability to meet adequately the theoretical challenges noted above, as well as in terms of the larger issue of making a meaningful contribution to human emancipation.

As I worked to assemble arguments in support of these conclusions, I benefited greatly from the work of earlier critics of positivism in International Relations theory.[6] Though some of them now advocate a postmodernism of which I remain wary, my indebtedness to this

4

group of thinkers is quite profound. At pivotal junctures encounters with the ideas of individuals such as Ashley, Cox, George, Frost, Linklater, and Walker helped provide answers, not only to specific queries about positivism, but also to larger questions about what form critical thinking could take in a discipline not noted for its openness to such an enterprise.

A final point needs to be made concerning the research strategy being adopted here. As already noted, this is a study in meta-theory. That is, this book concerns itself with the background of philosophical tenets and assumptions that provide rules for the construction of particular theories and a framework for the analysis of particular issues. As such, the focus of attention is the presuppositions of a critical International Relations theory rather than the details of its structure. Consequently, specific analyses of concrete issues in international politics will not be offered. Indeed, as will be noted in the concluding chapter, the translation of the meta-theoretical gains of the restructuring process into advances in the analysis of specific topics in international politics remains to be effected.

Methodology

Beyond the issue of research strategy, the methodology adopted in this study also bears noting. What will be undertaken here, in the effort to explore the issue of a (meta-)theoretical restructuring of International Relations theory, is what is referred to in the tradition of critical theory as an 'immanent critique' of the discipline. The method of 'immanent critique', which is central to the work of Hegel, and advocated by members of the Frankfurt School such as Max Horkheimer and Theodor Adorno,

> starts with the conceptual principles and standards of an object, and unfolds their implications and consequences. Then it re-examines and reassesses the object ... in light of these implications and consequences. Critique proceeds, so to speak, 'from within'.[7]

It is the methodology of 'immanent critique' which is responsible for the focus of this study on positivist epistemology. It is a common observation that International Relations has traditionally been pre-occupied with epistemological questions (how best to study world politics), often to the neglect of ontological ones (assumptions about the nature of the world). Accordingly, in keeping with the notion that

5

critique is most effective when it proceeds 'from within', epistemology is the principal focus here. In this way, it is hoped that the analysis offered here is less likely to be rejected with the charge that 'its concepts impose irrelevant criteria of evaluation'.[8]

At the same time, it must be stressed that adopting the method of 'immanent critique' has implications not just for what issues are taken as the focus of discussion, but also for how those issues are treated. In simplest terms, the *telos* of immanent critique is positive: it leads to a reassessment of the object in question with an eye toward its transformation. If carried out properly,

> a new understanding of the object is generated – a new comprehension of contradictions and possibilities ... The object's view of itself is contradicted by its effective actuality. Through reflection and critique, it can become aware of its own limitations; that is, that it fails by its own standards. Through this awareness it develops and becomes open to radical change.[9]

In terms of International Relations theory, then, an immanent critique of positivist epistemology leads well beyond conventional conclusions about the need to refine techniques of information gathering and processing. In raising questions about issues such as the status of norms, of the human subject, and of reason/truth, it directs our attention to the imperative for a fundamental rethinking of all of the assumptions upon which the discipline rests: ontological as well as epistemological.

Politico-philosophical specificity of the study at hand

Before moving to an overview of chapter content, it is important to draw attention to the specificity of this study, particularly as regards its politico-philosophical orientation.

It is one of the core arguments of this work that the 'view from nowhere', which serves as a regulative ideal for much of mainstream International Relations scholarship, is not only not attainable but a dangerous illusion; that all theoretical efforts proceed from and embody a perspective. This holds equally for the study at hand. Specifically, the argument regarding a 'restructuring' of International Relations theory which is advanced here is framed in the terms of the tradition of Western Marxism (including Gramsci), and in particular the variant known as the 'Frankfurt School'.

Other critically oriented traditions exist within the discipline, of course, and they cannot be overlooked. Two in particular – those of postmodern International Relations theory and feminist International Relations theory – are considered in terms of their contribution to the emancipatory restructuring process identified in contemporary theorizing.[10] For despite suffering from important limitations – and I will argue this holds especially true for postmodern International Relations theory[11] – it must also be recognized that the rise of these traditions over the last decade is some of the strongest evidence for the critical restructuring of International Relations theory.

Chapter outline

On the basis of this brief discussion of research strategy, methodology, and specificity, I will now outline the course this book will follow. In chapter one, the inadequacy of contemporary theorizing in International Relations will be discussed. Specifically, it will be argued that in its failure to place the issue of human emancipation at the centre of theorizing, International Relations is missing an historic opportunity to contribute to the betterment – if not the very survival – of the human species. It is argued that if International Relations theory is to make a meaningful contribution to human emancipation, it will need to be fundamentally 'restructured' so as to incorporate the elements necessary for theorizing in terms of the goal of human emancipation. Drawing on the tradition of 'critical theory', three such elements are identified.

In chapter two, and as part of the effort to account for the absence of the elements which characterize 'critical theory' from theorizing about international relations, an examination of the dominant approach to the study of international politics – that of 'positivism' – is undertaken. Specifically, the central tenets and underlying assumptions of 'positivism' as an approach to the study of human society are identified.

In the three chapters which follow, each of the three elements which characterize critical theory is discussed in relation to contemporary theorizing about International Relations. In each case, the absence of the critical element is explained in terms of the predominance of the positivist approach. As a consequence, it is argued that part of the process of 'restructuring' International Relations theory in a critical fashion must involve a challenge to positivism itself.

However, the study goes beyond simply indicating the elements which must be integrated if International Relations is to be reconstituted as a critical discipline. Rather, in each case it is argued that the process of challenging positivism and of restructuring International Relations theory is already underway. Indeed, it is the central contention of this study that contemporary developments in the discipline which seem at first glance to be unrelated – if significant – challenges to positivist orthodoxy are, in fact, evidence of a profound process of theoretical 'restructuring': a 'restructuring' which is already taking International Relations theory in a more critical direction.

1   International Relations theory and the Aristotelian project

> Perhaps no event has had a more disastrous effect upon the development of political science than the dichotomy between political theory and political science. For it has made political theory sterile by cutting it off from contact with the contemporary issues of politics, and it has tended to deprive political science of intellectual content by severing its ties with the Western tradition of political thought, its concerns, its accumulation of wisdom and knowledge.
>
> Hans J. Morgenthau[1]

> To the extent that it is correct to speak of a crisis in science, that crisis cannot be separated from the general crisis.
>
> Max Horkheimer[2]

Theory and the 'global *polis*'

'The leading of a good and just life in the *polis*' was the 'Aristotelian *telos*' of all political inquiry.[3] Exploring and cultivating public awareness of the basis upon which the citizens of the *polis* might lead such a life – the 'Aristotelian project' – was the task of all responsible students of human society. No other justification for their activity as scholars and teachers was necessary, or, indeed, acceptable.

The nature of the *polis* was of central concern for those working within the Aristotelian project. In this regard, it is important to note that the *polis* was not so much a 'place' as a 'way of living'. As Hannah Arendt has argued, the Aristotelian conception of the *polis* was that of a very special and freely chosen form of political organization.[4] In short, the *polis* was more than just the locality in which citizens were to live – the polis was the 'moral–political order that rendered its citizens capable of leading a good and just life'.[5]

9

Central to this form of political organization was the understanding that to live in a *polis* meant that everything was decided through words and persuasion, and not through force and violence.[6] But the idea of the *polis* involved more than the simple absence of overt violence. It was also coterminous with the values of liberty and equality. The *polis* 'knew only equals' whose shared objective was 'neither to rule nor to be ruled'. And it was on this basis of equality that the realm of the *polis* was to be the 'sphere of freedom'.[7]

It should be noted, however, that equality between the members of the *polis* was not understood in terms of some objective quality of human beings located outside of history. It was viewed neither as a natural condition of human beings, nor as an attribute or right with which human beings have been endowed by their creator. Rather, this freedom-guaranteeing equality was seen as a function of the *polis* itself. In Arendt's words,

> Isonomy guaranteed ... equality, but not because all men were born or created equal, but, on the contrary, because men were by nature ... not equal, and needed an artificial institution, the *polis*, which ... would make them equal.[8]

It is clear then, that the *polis* was not a naturally existing locality. Nor should it be understood as a locality defined by fixed geographical boundaries. Rather, the *polis* was a socially created 'political space' whose dimensions were determined by the people participating in its creation. Notes Arendt, 'not Athens but the Athenians were the *polis*':[9]

> The *polis*, properly speaking, is not the city-state in its physical location; it is the organization of the people as it arises out of acting and speaking together, and its true space lies between people living together for this purpose, no matter where they happen to be. 'Wherever you go, you will be a *polis*': these famous words ... expressed the conviction that action and speech create a space between the participants which can find its proper location almost any time and anywhere.[10]

Arendt's point that the *polis* can be created by willing participants 'almost any time and anywhere' is an important one. It is also important to note that different times and historical contexts may require different conceptions of the spatial dimensions of the *polis*.

As was observed above, the function of the political arrangement known as the *polis* was to ensure the conditions necessary for the leading of a good and just life, a life encompassing the values of equality and freedom. It follows that to be capable of this, the *polis* 'must be coterminous with the minimum self-sufficient human reality'.[11]

During the time period of classical Greece, the small city-state was viewed as adequate to this task. In modern history, however, it has been considered that a *polis* of those dimensions can no longer suffice. For Hegel, writing at the beginning of the nineteenth century, the political institution which best conformed to the requirement of being 'coterminous with the minimum self-sufficient human reality' was that of the modern nation-state.[12] In contrast to the focus of the classical Greeks on their fellow citizens in the city-state, for thinkers such as Hegel – and especially for his followers, the Young Hegelians – it was the fellow citizens of one's nation-state who were to be of central concern to those committed to working within the Aristotelian project.

Even before Hegel's time, however, there were those openly questioning whether the modern nation-state was an adequate geopolitical container for the ideal of just human relationships. Perhaps one of the best representatives of this group was Immanuel Kant. What was innovative about Kant's approach to international politics was the substitution of 'human beings' for 'citizens' as the proper subjects of moral concern.[13] This substitution can be seen as an important step in the modern effort to redefine the Aristotelian project in more universal terms through the 'extension of the area of the common good'.[14]

This effort has taken on new impetus in the twentieth century. The threats to human well-being and autonomy posed by weapons of mass destruction, the ecological crisis, the systematic violation of human rights around the globe, and the growing disparity between rich and poor within an increasingly interdependent world economy, have been interpreted as requiring a supersession of the present world order, and as demanding a transformation of our most basic political categories.[15]

In a context in which the factors which will determine whether the human species will survive or perish, suffer or prosper, operate on a global scale, a good case can be made that the *polis* which is 'coterminous with the minimum self-sufficient human reality' is the planet itself. In short, the problems presently faced by the human species call out for the identification of the idea of the *polis* with the planet as a whole: a truly *global polis*.

As was noted at the beginning of this essay, the Aristotelian project involved theoretical reflection on – as well as cultivation of public awareness of – the conditions necessary for the leading of a 'good and just life in the *polis*', where the *polis* is defined as a 'sphere of freedom' in which community life is oriented to promoting equality between its members. It follows that if we are now to speak of a global *polis*, distinguished by the presence of global-level threats to human well-being, then we shall require a body of theory capable of conceptualizing the Aristotelian project on a global scale and in terms of contemporary challenges. In short, what we require is nothing less than a body of theory which can provide us with a 'new, encompassing language for political discourse on a planetary scale'.[16]

It could be argued that the most logical candidate for such a task is 'International Relations theory'. Moreover, it is worth noting that prominent theorists within this discipline have, with increasing frequency, been claiming just such a role for International Relations theory. In the words of Stanley Hoffmann:

> the architectonic role Aristotle attributed to the science of politics might well belong today to International Relations, for these have become in the twentieth century the very condition of our daily life. To philosophise about the ideal state in isolation, or to theorise about political systems in the abstract, has become almost meaningless.[17]

Indeed, a number of prominent International Relations scholars would seem to share classical theory's concern with contributing to the quality of human life. 'An introduction to the study of International Relations in our time', writes Karl Deutsch, 'is an introduction to the art and science of the survival of mankind'.[18] 'We study world politics', affirms Robert Keohane, 'because we think it will determine the fate of the earth'.[19] And 'specialists in world affairs', argues J. David Singer, 'have a special responsibility ... to address the major problems confronting the global village'.[20]

Yet one cannot but be disappointed upon examining the theoretical content of the discipline of International Relations in light of the idea of the *polis*. For theory which is oriented toward making human relations at the global level a 'sphere of freedom' must, in light of the considerable constraints on human autonomy, be theory which addresses the question of human emancipation. Lamentably, it is just this kind of theory which is so notably absent from the discipline of

International Relations. As Andrew Linklater notes in his review of the discipline,

> Little elaboration is needed ... of the fact that theory committed to the reduction or eradication of constraints upon human autonomy remains poorly developed within the field of International Relations.[21]

If Linklater's assessment is accurate – and it is a central contention of this study that it is – then we are forced to confront an unattractive conclusion. Despite its *prima facie* suitability for a global analysis, and despite the professed desire of a number of its leading scholars, in its present state International Relations theory is incapable of making a meaningful contribution in the terms set out by the Aristotelian project. Furthermore, it is equally clear that if a meaningful contribution is to be made, a fundamental transformation of the discipline – a 'restructuring' of International Relations theory which will place the question of human emancipation at centre-stage – is required.

Contemplating the idea of a 'restructuring' of International Relations theory raises two important questions. First, there is the question of *why* 'theory committed to the reduction or eradication of constraints upon human autonomy remains poorly developed within the field of International Relations': that is, why are the defining characteristics of emancipatory theory absent from International Relations theory? Secondly, there is the question of the future evolution of International Relations in relation to the Aristotelian project: that is, what are the prospects that International Relations theory can be 'restructured' so as to incorporate the defining characteristics of emancipatory theory into the discipline?

It is the task of the chapters that follow to provide answers to these two questions. Before proceeding any further however, a third question must first be addressed. It concerns the nature of theorizing that does place the issue of the 'reduction or eradication of constraints upon human autonomy' at the centre of its concerns: that is, what are the defining characteristics of emancipatory theory? The remainder of this chapter will concern itself with providing an answer to this question.

Human emancipation and the tradition of critical theory

As a means to identify the defining characteristics of emancipatory theory, I will focus on one tradition of political theory which has

13

consistently placed the question of human freedom at the centre of its concerns: that of 'critical' theory. By critical theory is meant that tradition of theorizing which has its roots in the Enlightenment notion of 'critique'.[22]

In fact, the term 'critique' itself predates the Enlightenment. It was first used by Humanists and Reformers during the Reformation period who were engaged in biblical criticism, and described the 'art of informed judgment appropriate to the study of ancient texts'.[23] This 'art' was used to uncover hidden assumptions and, above all, to debunk claims to authority. In the pre-Enlightenment context of the Reformation, then, critique served as a powerful weapon in the hands of those engaged in the criticism of established ecclesiastical practice. Thus, from the beginning, the tradition of theorizing associated with the notion of critique served as an instrument for the delegitimization of established power and privilege.[24]

It was in the context of the Enlightenment, however, that the 'art of critique' assumed its mature form. For it was then that critique began to enjoy a status independent of the authoritative scriptures to which it was applied. Increasingly, critique was adopted as a criterion of truth, where truth was defined as the product of clear and rational thinking. Indeed, much to the chagrin of all of the contending factions during the Reformation, the critical definition of truth began to assume a place in opposition to that of 'truth from revelation'.

Indeed, critique was now equated with the 'essential activity of reason' itself. As such, it claimed to stand in judgment of 'all spheres of life',[25] including the political sphere. Indeed, in the context of the Enlightenment, critique was viewed to have acquired 'public force',[26] and became virtually synonymous with the existence of an informed, critical public.[27] And it was in the Enlightenment context that critique – in its ability to combat 'unfreedom' rooted in false beliefs and distorted thinking – became inextricably linked to the project of human emancipation.

It is thus understandable that Immanuel Kant asserts, in the preface to the *Critique of Pure Reason* (1781),[28] that his time should be understood as no less than the 'age of critique'.[29] Nor is there any question that Kant shared this Enlightenment orientation:

> Enlightenment is mankind's release from its self-incurred tutelage. Tutelage is mankind's inability to make use of its understanding without direction from another. Self-incurred is this tutelage when

its cause lies not in lack of reason but in the lack of resolution and courage to use it without direction from another. *Sapere aude!* 'Have courage to use your own reason!' – that is the motto of enlightenment.[30]

Indeed, Kant's own contributions to the notion of critique were considerable, and the Kantian element in the tradition of critical theory is fundamental. In keeping with the Enlightenment notion that 'unfreedom' was rooted in false beliefs and distorted thinking, for Kant, critique was defined first and foremost as reflection on conditions of reliable knowledge for human beings possessing the faculties of knowing, speaking, and acting. Specifically, Kant's central question, which served as the guiding thread to his theorizing in the *Critique of Pure Reason*, was the following: what are the conditions of human knowledge through which our experience of the world around us is possible?

Kant's philosophical adversaries, the empiricists Locke and Hume, argued that inquiry must be restricted to the 'contents' of consciousness: that is, the world experienced through sense impressions. Kant did not deny these 'contents'. But where he diverged from the empiricists was in insisting that the organization and interpretation of these 'contents' also bore examination. For the fact is that only an incoherent profusion of impressions and sensations are given in perception. And yet, noted Kant, we always perceive the world as a realm of ordered things.[31]

The fact that we do so, argued Kant, can only be understood in terms of the creative and ordering function of human consciousness. Thus, in contrast to the empiricists, who affirmed that reliable knowledge – to the degree to which it was attainable at all – was the product of a passive reception of sense impressions, Kant affirmed that empirical reality is always apprehended 'in a mediated fashion by means of *a priori* categories of the mind'.[32] In short, argued Kant, while reality is not a pure construct of mind, knowledge is dependent on the 'active, synthetic function of the mind'.[33]

Kant's assertion of the need for theorizing about the origins and nature of knowledge, as well as his emphasis on the creative role of human consciousness, was further developed by the second major Enlightenment contributor to the tradition of critical theory: George Wilhelm Friedrich Hegel. It should be noted that for Kant, the creative role of human consciousness in the ordering of perceived reality and the production of knowledge was framed in terms of a self-contained and unchanging transcendental subject. Furthermore, in Kant's terms, the need for theorizing about the origins and nature of knowledge was limited to a concern with 'epistemology', narrowly conceived.[34] Hegel's contribution to the development of the tradition of critical theory involved a radical transformation of both of these formulations.

First, Hegel rejected Kant's notion of a self-contained and unchanging transcendental subject, a formulation corresponding to the liberal conception of the autonomous, atomized individual as the starting point for understanding human interaction and development. The problem with Kant's liberal-inspired formulation was that it did not recognize that society as an expression of the interaction of 'autonomous' individuals was itself historically contingent; that individuation which marks modernity is not a timeless state but a social process.[35]

It was thus Hegel's contribution that he underscored the fact of the 'intersubjective' and historically contingent nature of human identity and human consciousness. The synthesizing categories of the mind to which Kant had drawn attention – but for which he was unable to account theoretically[36] – were now understood as historically emergent intersubjective categories shared by mutually interdependent members of a community. Moreover, because these categories were now understood as products of an historical process, they were also seen to be subject to change and further evolution as human communities continued their struggle to comprehend and master a changing social environment of which they are, at one and the same time, the product and the creator. In short, argued Hegel, the criteria of reliable knowledge are themselves historically emergent social products.

In conjunction with, and as a consequence of, this first reformulation, Hegel redefined Kant's conceptualization of theoretical reflection on reliable knowledge as being limited to the concerns of 'epistemology'. For while not denying the importance of epistemological questions,[37] it was clearly one of Hegel's most important innovations that he relocated the question of epistemology within the context of the 'historical self-formative process' (*Bildungsprozeß*) noted above: an historical process whose endpoint was that of truth defined as self-realization.[38] In Hegel's words:

> the truth is the whole. The whole, however, is merely the essential nature reaching its completeness through the process of its own

development. Of the Absolute it must be said that it is essentially a result, that only at the end is it what it is in its very truth; and just in that consists its nature, which is to be actual, subject or self-becoming, self-development.[39]

The importance of this 'relocation' is central to the development of the problematic of human emancipation within the tradition of 'critique'. At the core of Hegel's theorizing is the Enlightenment position that a defining characteristic of human existence throughout history has been the presence within human communities of a system of constraints on human autonomy which are themselves humanly produced. However, because the true origins of these constraints are rarely recognized – because, for example, social distinctions are perceived to be part of nature, and thus 'naturally sanctioned' – constraints are seen as unchangeable. In short, it is the recurring misrecognition of the nature of socially constructed constraints on human autonomy which has to a great extent resulted in their persistence, and, as a consequence, in an alienated existence.

Yet Hegel also argued that an equally fundamental characteristic of human history and historically contingent rationality is the process of 'negation': that is 'the criticism in life and in thought of the constraints imposed by each of its specific historical forms'.[40] It was Hegel's contention that

> At each new stage in the self-development of consciousness, the subject reconstructs its self-understanding in relation to its past. This reconstruction involves the 'negation' of the old forms of conscious-ness, which are forms of, *and* attitudes toward, concrete life.[41]

It was this process of 'negation' that led to the recognition that history is nothing more than 'human practice'; that social relations have their source not in nature, but in that same practice, and thus may be 'determined by human deliberations'.[42] In short, affirmed Hegel, it was critical thinking that would promote the development of the 'species-powers' necessary to human freedom.

In this way, Hegel radicalized Kant's epistemological preoccupation by introducing the notion of a human subject who attains knowledge through a struggle for understanding and for recognition with others. With the notion of critique broadened to include 'the experience of an emancipation by means of critical insight into relationships of power, the strength of which lies, at least in part, in the fact that these relationships have not been seen through',[43] critical theory's task was extended to encompass reflection upon humanly produced systems of constraints on human liberty.[44] From this point on, critical theoretical reflection would be understood to involve more than the questions specific to epistemology narrowly defined: the 'critique of knowledge' (Kant) would be seen to '[entail] a critique of rational action or forms of life' (Hegel).[45]

Thus, it was in specifying the role of critique as more than 'negative judgement' – indeed, as playing a central and positive role in the historical movement from 'self-estrangement' to 'self-determination' – that Hegel reinforced the link between critical theory and the goal of human emancipation. Yet it was left to a third and final Enlightenment contributor to the tradition of critique – Karl Marx – to bring that tradition to its mature formulation.

To begin, there is no question that Marx identified himself with the tradition of critical theorizing begun by Kant and extended by Hegel.[46] It cannot be denied, for example, that 'the dominant characteristic of history as a history of human capacities or species-powers is reiterated within Marx's framework'.[47] Even after his break with the 'Young Hegelians', Marx retained the notion of critique as a process of theoretical reflection oriented toward human emancipation. As the Western Marxist philosopher Korsch has noted, it is not insignificant that Marx subtitled all of his major works as 'critique'.[48]

Notwithstanding his identification with the central emphasis of Kant, and especially Hegel, Marx did go beyond both of their conceptualizations to make a vital contribution to the evolution of the tradition of critical theory. The nature of his contribution grew out of his dissatisfaction with the highly 'speculative' nature of Hegel's philosophy as concerned the nature of the creative subject in history as well as the general path to human emancipation. We shall examine these two elements in turn.

The difficulty Marx saw in Hegel's theoretical formulation was that the human dimension of social and political life was subsumed within – and, indeed, subordinated to – the central and creative role of *'Geist'* (spirit). In place of the unfolding of the 'World Spirit', Marx underscored ' "sensuous human activity" through which labouring subjects regulate their material exchange process with nature and in so doing constitute a world'.[49] 'People make their own history', affirmed Marx, even if not under the circumstances of their choosing.[50] Thus one of Marx's primary contributions to the development of the critical tradition was to replace 'spirit' with thinking and acting human subjects as the creative force in history.

Marx also felt dissatisfaction with the path to emancipation outlined by Hegel. As was noted above, it was the central contention of Hegel's conception of critique that human unfreedom was rooted in 'false beliefs' (ideology). As a consequence, it was held that one had only to 'reform consciousness to set the individual on the path to autonomy'.[51]

While certainly accepting that false beliefs lay at the root of human alienation, Marx was clearly dissatisfied with the proffered solution. The problem with the Hegelian conceptualization, noted Marx, is that it is 'a merely theoretical emancipation'.[52] As such, it risked reducing the Enlightenment notion of emancipation as 'self-determination' to that of reconciliation with the status quo. In short, the major flaw in the Hegelian solution to the problem of unfreedom is that it left the real world untouched.

This was a major failing, for while Marx agreed that the reform of consciousness was a vital and necessary first step in overcoming alienated human existence, he also recognized that the goal of human emancipation required fundamental change in the way society was organized. And it was no doubt in response to this important limitation in Hegel's theoretical contribution that Marx formulated his well-known eleventh thesis on Feuerbach:

> The philosophers have only interpreted the world in different ways; the point, however, is to change it.[53]

In short, critique would be understood as more than theoretical reflection on epistemological concerns, and as even more than intellectual judgments on ideology. As a result of Marx's reformulation, critical theory would be understood in terms of practical political activity – undertaken by 'conscienticized' human agents – and oriented toward a radical transformation of society.[54]

On the basis of this admittedly schematic overview of the origins and evolution of the emancipation-oriented theoretical tradition associated with the notion of 'critique', we are now in a position to identify the defining characteristics of emancipatory theory.[55] Simply put, the defining characteristics of emancipatory theory are those core elements which together constitute the critical tradition. There are three.

The restructuring of International Relations theory

The first defining characteristic of emancipatory theory is that of 'theoretical reflexivity'. This concerns the notion, highlighted by Kant, and reaffirmed by Hegel and Marx, that theorizing which hopes to make a meaningful contribution to human emancipation cannot confine itself to an examination of the empirical, as important as that is. Emancipatory theory must also involve an on-going process of 'theoretical reflection on the process of theorizing itself'.

The second characteristic derives from the recognition, underscored by Kant, and broadened by Hegel and Marx, of the creative role of human consciousness: a role which goes beyond the process of knowledge production, narrowly defined, to include the constitution and transformation of modes of social and political life. It is the on-going attention to the constitutive and non-reductive power of human consciousness in dialectical interaction with the natural environment which stands as the second characteristic of emancipatory forms of theorizing.

And finally, in keeping with the general orientation of the Aristotelian project, emancipatory theory is characterized by its engagement in social criticism in support of practical political activity oriented toward societal transformation. Specifically, emancipatory theory seeks to promote a process of education and 'conscientization' among those poorly served by present social and political arrange-ments, through which the disadvantaged can empower themselves to effect radical social change. In short, emancipatory theory is characterized by the desire to serve as 'the self-clarification of the struggles and wishes of the age'.[56]

Conclusion

In this chapter we have accomplished two tasks. First, we have noted the failure of the discipline of International Relations to make a meaningful contribution in terms of the contemporary requirements of the Aristotelian project. Specifically, International Relations has been faulted for not having placed the issue of human emancipation at the centre of its theoretical concerns, a weakness all the more ironic in view of the clear interest of some of its leading theorists in promoting human welfare.

Secondly, we have examined a tradition of theorizing that has consistently placed the question of human emancipation at centre-stage: that of critical theory. In the process, we have identified the three 'critical' elements which characterize emancipatory theory: theoretical reflexivity, attention to the creative role of human consciousness, and a concern with social criticism in support of practical political activity oriented toward radical social change.

In the following chapters, it will be argued that if International Relations has not placed the question of human emancipation at the centre of its theoretical concerns, this can be best understood in terms of the traditional absence of the core elements of the theoretical tradition of 'critique'. Moreover, it will be argued that the absence of these 'critical' elements is not accidental. Specifically, it will be argued that the absence of these elements is a direct result of the predominance of a particular philosophy of science in the discipline of International Relations: that of positivism. Before the relationship between the presence of positivism and the absence of the elements of emancipatory (critical) theory can be understood, however, the characteristics of positivism must be identified. That is the task of the chapter which follows.

2   Defining positivism

It is the task of theory to detect in the welter of the unique facts of experience that which is uniform, similar, and typical. It is its task to reduce the facts of experience to mere specific instances of general propositions, to detect behind them the general laws to which they owe their existence and which determine their development.

Hans J. Morgenthau[1]

The question 'What is theory?' appears to pose no great problems for contemporary science. What counts for theory in customary research is the sum-total of propositions about a subject area that are connected to each other such that from a few one can derive the rest ... Theory is a store of knowledge in a form that makes it useful for the most thorough-going description of facts.

Max Horkheimer[2]

Introduction

Before proceeding any further it is important to have a clear idea of what is meant by a positivist approach in the context of the social sciences. This is a critical question and it is important to be clear about what is being argued here. To that end, it may be useful to begin by pointing out what is *not* being argued in this study.

First of all, it is not being argued that positivism can be understood in terms of the popular caricature identified with amoral, atheoretical 'number crunchers'. This popular caricature is inappropriate because many positivists have strong moral commitments and are quite concerned with theory. Furthermore, as will hopefully become clear, quantification is neither sufficient nor necessary for a study of the social world to qualify as positivist.

It will also not be argued that one can equate positivism in the social sciences with the work of self-designated positivists; such a strategy is simply too restrictive. It must be recognized that many social scientists are self-consciously 'agnostic' with regard to questions concerning the philosophy of (social) science. However, because individual scholars do not consciously identify themselves with the positivist approach does not mean that such an approach has not been adopted unconsciously. Moreover, whether or not positivism is consistently applied by specific individuals, it can still be argued that positivism is structuring the bulk of the research that is being undertaken through its generalized pervasiveness as the unspoken epistemological backdrop of the research efforts of the research community as a whole.

Consequently, were we to limit ourselves to those individuals who have self-consciously and rigorously pursued a positivist research agenda, the extent of positivism's influence on theorizing about international politics would be greatly underestimated. Of course, we cannot escape making reference to individual statements and analyses in the effort to show the predominance of positivism in the study of the social world. However, the point is what these statements/analyses say *in their combination* about the discipline in question, rather than whether the individual researchers to whom they are attached are self-conscious and consistent adherents of the positivist approach.

Finally, it will not be argued that positivism can be defined in terms of the specific methodological characteristics of one or another of the more well-known variants of positivism. This strategy is not useful for the simple reason that the positivist tradition has spawned many variants which often differ significantly in both methodology and research design, not to mention the fact that those variants are often applied in a non-rigorous manner. To identify positivism as a whole with one or another of its historically specific variants (or rather, a corrupted version thereof) would again be too restrictive, and would also lead to the misrecognition of the full extent of positivism's influence on contemporary social science.

Consequently, the strategy that will be adopted is the following. In the first part of this chapter, I will examine two distinct variants of the positivist tradition: (i) Comtean positivism – the earliest manifestation of the tradition dating from the nineteenth century, and (ii) logical positivism – perhaps the most fully developed and influential variant, dating from the first half of the twentieth century. What I shall be concerned with is something more probing than a surface-level description of these two variants of positivism. What I shall be attempting to capture are the central tenets common to these and indeed to all other variants of positivism – the central tenets that together constitute 'the positivistic logic of investigation'.[3]

Following the determination of these core tenets, I will proceed to a discussion of their underlying assumptions. The identification of these assumptions is crucial, as it is the task of later chapters to cast doubt on the core tenets of positivism by challenging the validity of the assumptions on which they rest. In a context in which positivism continues to form the unquestioned backdrop of academic discourse, it is only by exposing the limitations of positivism that a space can be created for alternative forms of theorizing about international politics.

Comtean and logical positivism

The positivist approach to the study of society has a long history within the social sciences, spanning almost two centuries. It has its roots in the early part of the nineteenth century in the work of Auguste Comte. Comte envisaged three distinct types of knowledge – theological, metaphysical and 'positive' – corresponding to three stages in the evolution of human society: primitive, intermediary, and scientific, respectively. Thus for Comte 'positive' knowledge – from which the 'positivist' tradition takes its name – was seen to correspond in temporal terms to the rise of 'scientific' (industrial) society.

According to Comte, the positivist approach would yield a methodologically unified conception of science which would provide true, objective knowledge in the form of causal laws of phenomena, derived from observation.[4] For our purposes, three aspects of this conceptualization should be noted.

First, positive knowledge would be 'true' in that it would correspond to empirical experience (facts). In this Comte was clearly influenced by seventeenth-century empiricists such as David Hume.[5]

Secondly, positive knowledge would be 'objective' in that its grasp of the facts would be achieved without reference to (and without being subject to the distorting influence of) normatively oriented theological and metaphysical ideologies.[6]

24

And finally, positivism as an approach would be 'methodologically unified' in that it is held to be as well-suited to the study of the social world as it is to the natural world. It was Comte's view that each of the individual sciences must progress through a series of stages before achieving positive, scientific knowledge. And while it was the destiny of the science of society – 'sociology' (the term was Comte's) – to be the last to do so, its attainment of the positive knowledge was just as certain as that of the other sciences.

It cannot be denied that Comte's views were very influential in the nineteenth century; his concern with identifying universal laws operating in human society caught the imagination of a number of students of human affairs. Marx and Engels, for example, despite holding grave reservations about Comte's politics, shared his concern with uncovering the 'natural' laws of human social development.[7]

Nonetheless, Comte's views suffered from a number of imprecisions and even internal contradictions.[8] For that reason, they were to give way in the early part of the twentieth century to a new variant of positivism – 'logical positivism'. Logical positivism arose in the 1920s in Austria (the Vienna Circle), Germany (the Berlin School) and Poland, and quickly became dominant. Many of its principal theorists, however, such as Rudolf Carnap, Herbert Feigl, Hans Reichenbach and Carl Hempel, moved to the United States with the rise of Nazism.[9] Furthermore, many of the logical positivists were physicists and mathematicians, highly admiring of the new physics (relativity theory and quantum mechanics), who were concerned to explore the nature of science and, above all, to demonstrate what made it a reliable source of knowledge.

The adjectival modifier 'logical' in logical positivism indicates how this variant of positivism attempted to overcome the limitations of Comte's approach. What marked the work of the logical positivists was the central role played by symbolic logic, as developed by Russell and Frege.[10] By means of symbolic logic this group of philosophers attempted to purge the last vestiges of metaphysics from the positivist legacy (for which they blamed, in large part, Comte himself)[11] by providing a precise, formal rendering of the structure of science.

The emphasis on symbolic logic gave rise to three distinctive aspects of logical positivism: (i) the referential theory of meaning; (ii) the deductive–nomological method of explanation and the related hypothetico-deductive model of justification; and (iii) the axiomatic view of theories. These three aspects will be treated in turn.[12]

25

The logical positivists located many of the problems and uncertainties of science, especially those associated with the social sciences, in the unclear use of language.[13] Scientific language must be governed by strict rules of meaning, argued the logical positivists. In the absence of such rules, confusion reigns and scientists end up producing utterly meaningless statements. In the context of scientific discourse, a meaningless statement was worse than incorrect – it was not understandable.[14]

This raises the question of the criteria for meaningful statements. In their discussion of proper rules of meaning, the logical positivists followed Comte (and the classical empiricists) in linking knowledge to the empirical realm. There was an important innovation in their approach, however. Previously, ideas had played a central role in positivist and classical empiricist analysis; ideas were viewed as units of thinking and were considered to be the 'causal products of sensory experience'.[15] For the logical positivists, in contrast, ideas were 'fuzzy entities'. And it was for that reason that ideas were replaced by 'linguistic entities' – sentences and words – as the basic 'vehicles of meaning'.[16]

To explain how these linguistic entities were related to the empirical realm, the logical positivists advanced the 'referential theory of meaning'.[17] At the centre of this theory stood the 'verifiability principle',[18] according to which 'the meaning of a sentence was the set of conditions that would show that the sentence was true'.[19] In its simplest terms, the verifiability principle stipulated that 'a statement makes sense only if, and to the extent that, its empirical reference can be firmly corroborated'.[20] Every 'meaningful problem', affirmed Vienna Circle member Moritz Schlick, would be solved through the process of verification. And this process, wrote Schlick,

> in which the path to the solution finally ends is always of the same sort: it is the occurrence of a definite fact that is confirmed by observation, by means of immediate experience. In this manner the truth (or falsity) of every statement, of daily life or science, is determined.[21]

The logical positivists argued further that meaningful sentences could be separated into two classes. The first class of sentences – termed synthetic statements – were sentences which could be directly verified through experience. Although there was some disagreement about what kind of sentences belonged in this class, by and large logical positivists accepted sentences which referred to physical states of the world as being synthetic statements.[22]

However, there was another class of meaningful sentences – known as analytic statements – which could not be directly verified in terms of the empirical realm. Sentences containing theoretical or definitional terms which referred directly neither to empirical data nor to observable objects, for example, fell into this class. Yet it was also true that such sentences played an important role (that is, they had meaning) in scientific discourse. For that reason, the logical positivists tried to determine ways in which the truth or falsity of sentences using theoretical or definitional terms (analytic statements) could be verified indirectly by means of sentences which did refer directly to the empirical realm (synthetic statements).

In sum, it was the self-designated task of logical positivism

> to arrange all meaningful problems of cognition under two rubrics: they either concern analytical truths in the sense of a tautological explication of sign rules within a linguistic system; or else they deal with synthetic (aposteriori) statements in which case they must be anchored in extra-linguistic states of affairs denoted by language.[23]

The key to linking the two domains was provided by symbolic logic, which was employed to 'translate' analytic statements into synthetic statements. These translations generally consisted of 'biconditional sentences' in which one statement (the analytic statement) was held to be true if and only if the other (synthetic) statement was found to be true (in other words, if it conformed to the facts).[24]

Ultimately, the requirement that theoretical/definitional analytical statements have to be translatable into empirical synthetic statements was found to be too difficult to satisfy completely. Some theoretical terms can be translated in more than one way, and some seem not to be translatable at all.[25] Nonetheless, it can be argued that this criterion has remained regulative for individuals working within a positivist framework, premised as that framework is on the referential theory of meaning.

Finally, it is important to note the status of those sentences which do not fall into the two aforementioned categories. Such sentences include statements of a normative nature (e.g., 'freedom is good'). In terms of the referential theory of meaning, such statements were not so much wrong as 'meaningless'; not so much incorrect as 'empty sounds'.[26]

27

Of course logical positivists conceded that 'meaningless statements' were capable of playing an important role in eliciting emotional responses or provoking human action. But, maintained the logical positivists, that kind of role was possible only outside the realm of scientific discourse. In the realm of scientific discourse the concern is that of truth – of distinguishing between true and false statements – a concern which requires that all statements be meaningful in order to be assessable. Non-meaningful discourse (e.g., normative discourse) might be 'effective' in some contexts, but from the perspective of science it could only ever be confused discourse.[27]

But the logical positivists went beyond simply explicating criteria for making meaningful statements. Their central concern, like Comte before them, was to explain events in the empirical realm and to predict their future occurrence.[28] This raises the issue of what constitutes an adequate explanation in logical positivist terms, and how accurate predictions are possible. The logical positivist answers to these questions bring us to the second distinctive aspect of their formulation of the positivist approach: the deductive–nomological model of explanation, and the related hypothetico-deductive model of theory development.

In logical positivist terms, events in the empirical realm are held to be instances of observable regularities. These regularities, moreover, are held to be independent of time, place, and the human observer. Thus in answer to the question of the nature of adequate explanation for such an event, logical positivists argued that 'explaining an event consisted of deriving a statement describing that event from state-ments of scientific laws and statements describing antecedently known empirical facts (initial conditions)'.[29]

This view of explanation came to be known as the deductive–nomological or 'covering law' form of explanation. In simplest terms, an occurrence in the observable empirical realm is held to have been 'explained' once it has been identified as a manifestation of a regularity and has been subsumed under a general 'covering law' which specifies the causal determinants of the occurrence in question. In the words of Karl Popper:

> To give a causal explanation of an event means to deduce a statement which describes it, using as premises of the deduction one or more universal laws, together with certain singular statements, the initial conditions ... The initial conditions describe what is usually called the 'cause' of the event in question.[30]

The exact nature of these laws is clearly specified by logical positivism. Laws are conditional statements of the form 'if 'x' happens, 'y' (will) happen(s)'. As to statements describing initial conditions, these statements tell us that 'x' has happened.[31]

As noted by Brian Fay, the relationship between the variables specified by the law must satisfy three conditions:

i) the relationship must be invariable
ii) one variable must temporally precede, or at least be simultaneous with, the other
iii) the relationship must be asymmetrical, such that the occurrence of one (the independent) variable induces the occurrence of the other (dependent) variable, while the reverse is not true.[32]

In sum, notes Fay, covering laws which are causal in form 'state an invariable sequential order of dependence between kinds of states of affairs'.[33] And it should be noted that this form marks a law as positivist whether the law specifies individual variables or whether it is probabilistic in form, specifying the invariant relationships among mass events.[34]

How then does one go about developing laws to explain instances of empirical regularities? The answer provided by the logical positivists is that of the hypothetico-deductive method. According to this method, the scientist starts with an event that requires explanation. S/he then develops an hypothesis to account for its occurrence which – if true – can be used to derive a general covering law. This hypothesis is then tested against changed initial conditions. If the predictions stemming from the hypothesis are true, the hypothesis is confirmed.[35]

It should be noted here that positivism concerns itself not at all with the question of *where* the hypothesis comes from, or how the individual scientist arrives at the explanatory hypothesis in question. The speculative process which underlies hypothesis formulation belongs, according to the positivist approach, to the 'context of discovery' – a context potentially of interest to psychologists, but not really of any relevance to science. What is of relevance to science is the 'context of justification' – that is, the context in which strict methodological procedures must be followed in order to ensure that the testing of a given hypothesis against the facts is done properly.[36]

The point can be made clearer with an example from the natural sciences. Suppose that we are interested in explaining the boiling of water. One possible hypothesis to account for that event is one which relates the boiling of water to its temperature. Specifically, one might hypothesize that if water attains a temperature of 100 degrees Celsius, it will boil.[37] We might then test this hypothesis against varying initial conditions (i.e., different temperatures). If we find through such testing that, all things being equal, water boils when the temperature rises to 100 degrees Celsius, and if, moreover, experimentation indicates it always does so, we can consider the hypothesis to be confirmed.[38]

Now a confirmed hypothesis does more than account for why water has boiled in the past; it also allows us to predict when it will do so in the future. To understand why this is so, it is necessary to appreciate the unique nature of the deductive–nomological form of explanation. In fact, the positivist covering law-centred form of explanation postulates a 'structural identity' of explanation and prediction.[39] Since an empirical event is held to be explained once it has been identified as a regularity independent of time, place and observer, and can be derived from a general covering law, the same covering law will serve to predict its reoccurrence in the future.

An hypothesis which can be shown to be true through testing satisfies a necessary condition to be considered a 'covering law'. But while correspondence with the empirical world is a necessary condition for being considered a law, it is not sufficient. Bechtel provides a good example of why this is the case:

> if it were true that I only carried $1 bills in my wallet, then the following would be a true general statement: for all 'x', if 'x' is a bill in my wallet, then it is a $1 bill. But this intuitively is not a law. The reason is that there does not seem to be any reason except chance or my perversity for me to carry only $1 bills in my wallet. It is commonly thought that laws are more than general statements that happen to be true. We think they tell us something about the limits of how things *must be*.[40]

This then raises the question of how the logical positivists differentiated between *bona fide* laws and 'accidental generalizations'. The answer they provided to this question brings us to the third distinctive characteristic of logical positivism: the axiomatic account of theories.

Put simply, logical positivists differentiated between laws and accidental generalizations by arguing that laws, unlike accidental generalizations, are grounded in scientific theories. In fact, argue logical positivists, just as events are 'explained' in terms of (i.e., derived from) laws, so laws themselves are explained in terms of (i.e., derived from) theories. Indeed, the very definition of a scientific theory offered by logical positivists was that of a 'structured network of statements from which one could derive specific laws'.[41]

An example of the kind of theory favoured by logical positivists is that of Euclidean geometry. At its core is a set of basic terms and postulates from which axioms can be derived. Drawing on this example, the logical positivists argued that scientific theories should also be conceived as deductive structures built around a core of basic terms and postulates. The axioms which could be derived from this core would be the specific laws.[42]

In short, argued the logical positivists, scientific theory should be conceptualized as an axiomatic structure. Moreover, to the extent that scientists can be taught to think of theory in these terms, science itself will benefit. Efforts to axiomatize existing theoretical explorations will serve to introduce more rigour and clarity into the theoretical enterprise. Moreover, axiomatization may help scientists to discover implications of their theories of which they were not aware, thus providing new opportunities for hypothesis testing.[43]

In sum, then, logical positivism distinguished itself as a systematic and extremely elegant scientific project. It is a project which advances a theory of meaning in which scientific discourse is grounded in the empirical realm, and which employs deduction to show how specific events could be explained by scientific laws. It is a project in which the role of confirmation in the verification of laws is specified, and in which scientific laws themselves are shown to be derivable from axiomatic theoretical structures. For all of these reasons, logical positivism became dominant in the first half of the twentieth century, and, with some modifications, remains the standard for the vast majority of working scientists.[44]

Despite these distinctive characteristics, however, it is clear that logical positivism stands firmly within the tradition that began with Auguste Comte. Commonalities between the earlier Comtean positivism and logical positivism exist in at least three important respects. First, logical positivists, like Comtean positivists, make the empirical, observable realm the focus of investigation. The development of positive knowledge is viewed as a cumulative process in which more and more events are identified as being manifestations of regularities and subsumed under general covering laws. And it is the direct correspondence of positivist theory to the empirical realm which guarantees the truth of that theory.

A second commonality between logical positivists and Comtean positivists is the conviction that positivist research methods are as well suited to the study of the social world as they are to the study of the natural world. Indeed, some logical positivists went beyond a methodological unity to espousing a substantive unity of science in which the laws of specialized disciplines (e.g., psychology, political science) are viewed as 'derivative laws which, in principle, can be derived from the most basic laws of physics', thereby opening the possibility that human sciences might one day be 'subsumed within physics as a special application of physical laws'.[45] In any case, it is clear that in terms of logical positivism, Comte's original dream of a true 'science of society' remains a regulative ideal.

And finally, logical positivists, like the Comtean positivists before them, affirmed that the knowledge developed by means of their approach was objective knowledge. It was objective in that it was uninfluenced (i.e., undistorted) by metaphysical concerns and, indeed, occupied a sphere separate and distinct from that inhabited by 'nonsensical' normative and value-oriented discourses.

Of course, the positivist tradition continued to evolve beyond the contours of logical positivism. Important contributions were made in the post-war period by Karl Popper and Imre Lakatos, especially as regards the question of confirmation/falsification of hypotheses and 'research programmes'.[46]

At the same time, however, the three commonalities just noted have remained fundamental elements of the positivist tradition in both its Popperian neo-positivist and, most recently, Lakatosian variants. As such, they will serve as guideposts in our effort to identify the basic tenets of the positivistic logic of investigation. It is to a discussion of those tenets – and of the assumptions that underlie them – that we now turn.

The positivistic logic of investigation: tenets and assumptions

Based on this, admittedly cursory review of two concrete variants of the positivist tradition, we can now specify more clearly the central tenets which together form the core of the contemporary 'positivistic logic of investigation' in the social sciences. In line with the three commonalities identified above, it will be argued that there are three.[47] They are (i) the tenet of 'truth as correspondence'; (ii) the tenet of the methodological unity of science; and (iii) the tenet of the value-free nature of scientific knowledge. These three tenets are themselves based upon three distinct assumptions. I shall proceed with a discussion of these three tenets – and their underlying assumptions – in turn.

The first tenet: truth as correspondence

This tenet is at the very core of the positivistic logic of investigation. According to this tenet, positive knowledge – in contrast to 'metaphysical' or 'theological' knowledge – is reliable because it corresponds directly to the observable, empirical realm. Moreover, it is that correspondence which guarantees the 'truth' of positive knowledge.

Of course, it is important to note that positivists recognize that the knowledge they generate may not now – nor perhaps ever – correspond perfectly to objective reality. Even so, the goal of perfect correspondence remains the regulative ideal.[48]

What then is the assumption underlying this tenet? In short, it is the assumption of the separation of subject and object. This assumption postulates the existence of a 'real world' – the 'object' – which is separate and distinct from the theoretical constructions of the (social) scientist – the subject. It is held, moreover, that the theoretical constructions of the subject can be formulated in terms of a non-idiosyncratic intersubjectively valid observation language which captures reality – the facts – in direct terms.[49] Indeed, it is because of the possibility of methodologically 'factoring out' the identities of the individual researcher that 'objective knowledge of an intersubjectively transmissible character in the social sciences' is at all possible.[50]

Thus for positivists, true knowledge – Comte's 'positive' knowledge – is held to be knowledge which conforms to (and derives its truth-value from) objective reality. And there is no question that this position is shared by positivists working in the social sciences. Empiricism, affirms political scientist Eugene Meehan, 'is the only epistemic base for human knowledge'.[51] The task of the political scientist, states David Easton, is the collection of the 'objective facts' of political activity, while the validity of observation statements 'is determined by the correspondence of a statement to reality'.[52] In short, asserts political scientist Robert Dahl, in a particularly straightforward restatement of the tenet of 'truth as correspondence' (and its assumption of the non-relevance of the identity of the observer): 'Whether [an empirical] proposition is true or false depends on the degree to which the proposition and the real world correspond.'[53]

The second tenet: the methodological unity of science

According to this tenet, the research methodology developed for the study of the natural world – a methodology which has proved extremely successful – is equally suited to the study of the social world.

What then is the assumption underlying this second tenet? Here the assumption is that of naturalism. That is, it is assumed that there is no difference between the social world and the natural world so fundamental that the approach developed to conduct a scientific analysis of the natural world is not appropriate to the social world.

It is an integral aspect of the assumption of naturalism that the social world contains the same kind of regularities as one finds in the natural world. In this case, necessitous 'behavioural regularities' are independent of time, place, and, consistent with the first assumption of the separation of the subject and object, observer.

Once again, there is no question that this second core tenet of positivism – and the assumption underlying it – is held by positivists active in the study of human society. In the words of political scientist George Catlin:

> There can be no science of politics unless there are these political uniformities, these constants of behaviour, which admit of formulation as laws. And [these laws are] as timeless as the laws of mechanics, holding for the human race wherever and whenever it is found. And men in so far as they obey these laws will act in as timeless a fashion as ... atoms act in their chemical combinations according to formula. We are looking for this and nothing else.[54]

Easton would concur: without the 'search for uniformities in political relations', and for 'various levels of generalizations', the 'development of research towards theory is ... retarded'. For, argues Easton, the central task of political science is to develop a 'general framework within which ... facts [can] acquire meaning to transcend any particular time and place'.[55]

It is the assumption of naturalism which accounts for the extent to which the proponents of the forms of positivism reviewed above – both Comtean positivism and logical positivism – take considerable inspiration from the natural sciences (physics in particular). And it is the assumption of naturalism as well which explains the confidence expressed by adherents of the positivist approach that progress, defined as the gradual accumulation of ever truer hypotheses and theories, will occur in the social sciences as it has in the natural sciences: through hypothesis testing and replication.

Thus it is that Popper notes the tremendous successes attained by modern physics since the time of Galileo. In biology too, notes Popper, since the time of Pasteur – the Galileo of biology – scientific advance has been the norm. Only the social sciences lag behind, observes Popper, for they 'do not as yet seem to have found their Galileo'.[56]

The reason for Galileo's absence in the social sciences – the explanation for 'the disappointing results of a discipline already twenty-five hundred years old' – argues Easton, is the reluctance to emulate the 'scientific method' championed by Galileo and his successors.[57] As a consequence, it is the adoption of that method that will allow the social sciences to achieve their fullest promise.[58] And with its adoption in the twentieth century, affirms Kaspar Naegele, 'The study of society as a cumulative and, therefore, scientific, enterprise, is under way.'[59]

The third tenet: the value-free nature of scientific knowledge

This tenet of the contemporary positivistic logic of investigation is composed of two parts. First, it affirms that knowledge produced through positivist methodology and research design is knowledge restricted to the realm of the objective (i.e., empirical) world. Thus scientific knowledge does not pronounce upon disputes in the non-factual realm for the simple reason that resolving normative questions is not within the competence of science.

Secondly, this tenet affirms that the knowledge produced through positivist methodology and research design is knowledge unaffected by the value commitments of the researchers themselves. As such, positive knowledge is held to be knowledge which can be accepted by scholars with varying value orientations, thereby providing a 'common ground' on which constructive scientific interaction can take place.

What then is the assumption underlying this third tenet? Underlying the tenet of the value-free nature of scientific knowledge is the assumption of the separation of fact and value. In short, positivism assumes that the factual and the normative can be separated into distinct realms, with science concerning itself with the former while judiciously avoiding pronouncing upon or being influenced by the latter. This separation is at the heart of the logical positivist endeavour to separate meaningful statements (relating to the factual) which fall within the purview of science, from 'meaningless' statements such as those pertaining to normative issues. It is also at the heart of the considerable efforts made by positivists to devise methodological techniques and research designs which can serve to 'filter out' the value-bias of the individual researcher.

Once again, there is no question that this tenet and assumption are shared by positivistically inclined social scientists. Thus traditional concepts such as freedom, equality, democracy, and the 'good and just life' must be purged from the field of political science, for not only are such concepts 'vague, ambiguous, difficult or impossible to operationalize, useless as a guide to empirical choice',[60] but they are 'value-laden' and thus 'provide the additional difficulty of conveying both factual and distinctly evaluative meanings in research which presumably seeks to be primarily empirical'.[61]

Of course it is undeniable that researchers themselves have value commitments which underlie the research in which they engage. Even so, responds Easton,

> The mere statement ... that values underlie all research, does not in itself lead to the inevitable conclusion that these values must, by virtue of their presence, influence this research. Conceivably they could be there, *but remain quite innocuous and even irrelevant.*[62]

And, in any case, the goal of a value-free science remains the norm.

But what of the place of values in explaining human behaviour? Is it not important to be able to treat normative concerns in so far as they influence social interaction? Indeed, it is, responds Easton, who holds out the possibility of studying values – in so far as people do 'hold values' – as 'social facts'.[63] At the same time, it is crucial to

recognize that the assumption of the positivist student of social life
is that

> values can ultimately be reduced to emotional responses conditioned
> by the individual's total life-experiences. In this interpretation,
> although in practice no one proposition need express either a pure
> fact or a pure value, facts and values are logically heterogeneous.
> The factual aspect of a proposition refers to a part of reality; hence it
> can be tested by reference to the facts. In this way we check its truth.
> The moral aspect of a proposition, however, *expresses only the*
> *emotional response of an individual to a state of real or presumed facts.*[64]

The positivist position is clear. Values as 'emotional responses' – as
'social facts' – have meaning and can be used to generate knowledge.
But what of value questions outside of the realm of facts? Here
positivist social scientists fall into two camps. In the first and smaller
camp are those who, starting from the premise that 'Knowledge is not
knowledge until it has been substantiated, using the procedures
which have been labelled "scientific method"',[65] argue that value
questions debated outside of the realm of facts are meaningless. This
position, however, while a popular one during the reign of logical
positivism, has more recently fallen into some disrepute.

In the second and numerically larger camp, one finds positivists
who, while continuing to affirm that scientific knowledge is value-free
knowledge based on facts and validated by means of the 'scientific
method', nonetheless hold out the possibility that theorizing which
does not make a claim to science and which restricts itself to the
treatment of normative issues may have something to contribute as
well.[66] Indeed, it is the widespread acceptance that this position has
achieved in the positivist-dominated era that lends credence to the
argument that the very enterprise of 'normative theory' – as something distinct from that of 'scientific theory' – is a creation of
positivism itself.[67]

In sum, the tenet of the value-free nature of scientific knowledge,
and the assumption of the separation of fact and value underlying it,
insists that the competence of science lies in the analysis of objective
reality alone – the 'is' and not the 'ought'. And should one desire to
go beyond the realm of facts, even the most generous of positivists
will feel obliged to point out that in so doing one moves beyond the
realm of science as well. Moreover, even if they are of the opinion
that normative issues are worthy of study and analysis, their positivist

counsel may well be the following: 'These are philosophical questions better left to the philosophers.'[68]

Conclusion

To summarize, we have established that the logic of investigation of present-day positivism comprises three basic tenets: (i) truth as correspondence; (ii) the methodological unity of science; and (iii) the value-free nature of scientific knowledge. These three tenets rest, in turn, upon three basic assumptions: (i) the separation of subject and object; (ii) naturalism; and (iii) the separation of fact and value. Finally, we have established that these three tenets and their underlying assumptions are shared by positivist social scientists.

With this as background, we are now in a position to understand how the predominance of positivism in the discipline of International Relations has inhibited International Relations theory from developing as critical theory. The exact nature of the relationship between the dominance of positivism in International Relations theory and the absence of the defining characteristics of critical theory noted in the preceding chapter will be explored in the chapters which follow.

Finally, to the extent that this study is successful in demonstrating that a link exists between the dominance of positivism and the absence of critical theorizing, it is clear that if a 'space' is to be created for a more critical approach to the study of international relations – if International Relations theory is to be 'restructured' in a more critical fashion – then positivism itself will have to be challenged. It is thus the task of the next three chapters to show not only how the predominance of positivism in International Relations has impeded the development of critical forms of theorizing, but also to detail how the challenging of positivism and the restructuring of International Relations theory has already begun.

3   Reflexivity and International Relations theory

The 'personal equation' of the political scientist both limits and directs his scholarly pursuits. The truth which a mind thus socially conditioned is able to grasp is likewise socially conditioned. The perspective of the observer determines what can be known and how it is to be understood.   Hans J. Morgenthau[1]

'That we disavow reflection *is* positivism.'   Jürgen Habermas[2]

Introduction

We are now in a position to begin to address the central contention of this study. Specifically, at several points in this book, the following two arguments have been advanced. First, it has been suggested that the absence of the 'critical' elements which constitute emancipatory theory from the discipline of International Relations can be explained in terms of the predominance of positivism in International Relations theory. Secondly, it has been suggested that the predominance of positivism in International Relations theory is no longer unchallenged; that the prospects for incorporating the elements which distinguish emancipatory theory are improving. In sum, it is being suggested that there are signs that International Relations theory is in the process of being 'restructured' in a fundamental, 'critical' fashion, and that as a consequence, the potential for the discipline of International Relations to make a meaningful contribution in terms of the contemporary requirements of the Aristotelian project – a contribution to human emancipation – are better now than they have been for some time.

It is the task of this chapter and the two which follow to develop and substantiate these arguments. This chapter will focus on the question of 'theoretical reflexivity' – one of three 'critical' elements which constitute emancipatory theory. To that end, we shall proceed as follows. In the first part of this chapter, I will define more fully the notion of theoretical reflexivity as well as explain its essential incompatibility with positivist social science, including positivist International Relations theory. I will do this by relating the core elements of reflexivity to the positivist understanding of theory and knowledge, paying particular attention to the first of the three central tenets of the positivist approach: that of 'truth as correspondence'.

Then, in the second part of this chapter, I will explore the question of theoretical reflexivity in terms of International Relations theory. I will show how recent developments in positivist International Relations theory both reflect the influence of themes in contemporary social and political theory as well as underscore the continuing hegemony of positivist categories. Perhaps even more importantly, however, I will show that developments in social and political theory which have led to a questioning of positivism and a simultaneous opening to theoretical reflexivity also have their parallel in International Relations theory, albeit at the margins of the discipline. As a consequence, it is concluded that notwithstanding the fact that '[f]or many years the international relations discipline has had the dubious honour of being among the least self-reflexive of the Western social sciences',[3] the prospects for the development of theoretically reflexive International Relations theory are not as limited as they might at first appear.

Defining theoretical reflexivity

As was noted in chapter one, theoretical reflexivity can be defined in general terms as 'theoretical reflection on the process of theorizing itself'. It is important to recognize that within the parameters of this general definition, at least three core elements can be identified: (i) self-consciousness about underlying premises; (ii) the recognition of the inherently politico-normative dimension of paradigms and the normal science tradition they sustain; and (iii) the affirmation that reasoned judgments about the merits of contending paradigms are possible in the absence of a neutral observation language. These three

reflexivity takes one almost immediately to meta-theory

elements will be treated in turn. Furthermore, in the effort to show the essential incompatibility of a fully reflexive orientation with positivism, each element will be related to the positivist conception of theory and knowledge.[4]

Being aware of the underlying premises of one's theorizing is the first core element of theoretical reflexivity. That is, theoretical reflexivity is understood to involve attention to, and disclosure of, the too-often unstated presuppositions upon which theoretical edifices are erected.

If reflexivity were limited to this first element, then the positivist forms of theorizing which have dominated the discipline of International Relations would qualify with little difficulty as reflexive forms of theory; positivist notions of theory require that the sum total of generalizations be derived axiomatically from *clearly identified starting assumptions*. It is the presence of the two additional elements, however, which are incompatible with – and indeed, emerged from challenges to – positivist forms of theory that makes reflexivity a virtual antonym of positivism.

The second element of reflexivity is the recognition of the inherently politico-normative content of paradigms and the normal science traditions they generate. To understand the sense in which this element of reflexivity stands in opposition to positivist theorizing, it is important to recall the first tenet of the positivist tradition: that of 'truth as correspondence'.

As will be recalled from our discussion in the last chapter, 'truth as correspondence' is one of three core tenets of positivism.[5] That is, positivism stipulates that theoretical explanations will be true to the extent that they accurately reflect empirical reality; to the extent that they correspond to the facts.

It will also be recalled that this tenet rests upon a particular assumption: that of the separation of subject and object, of observer and observed. In other words, the tenet of 'truth as correspondence' assumes that through the proper application of research design and techniques, the researcher(s) can be 'factored out', leaving behind a description of the world 'as it truly is'. In short, the tenet of 'truth as correspondence' is the expression of the goal of rendering science a 'process without a subject'.

The consequence of this tenet and of this assumption is that a number of problematic issues are swept aside. In making the separation of subject and object a defining condition of science, the positivist approach ignores the active and vital role played by the community of researchers in the production and validation of knowledge. It ignores the fact that the standards which define 'reliable knowledge' are dependent upon their acceptance and application by a research community.[6]

As a result, a number of important questions not only go unanswered – they are never raised. They include questions of the historical origin and nature of the community-based standards which define what counts as reliable knowledge, as well as the question of the merits of those standards in the light of possible alternatives. These questions do not arise in positivist-inspired theorizing because the central standard of scientific truth – that of truth as correspondence – is seen to belong not to a time-bound human community of scientific investigators, but to an extra-historical natural realm. In short, the knowledge-defining standard of positivism is understood to be 'Nature's own'.[7]

In contrast, a theoretically reflexive orientation is one whose starting point stands in radical opposition to that of positivism in that it rejects the notion of objective standards existing independently of human thought and practice. In this, reflexively oriented theorists draw philosophical sustenance from the efforts to develop a post-positivist philosophy of science associated with the work of Kuhn and Feyerabend, as well as the linguistic turn in social and political theory, manifest in the Wittgensteinian analysis of 'language games', neo-pragmatist renditions of Gadamerian 'philosophical hermeneutics', and Foucault's analysis of power–knowledge discourses.[8] As different as these approaches are, all serve to undermine the assumption that it is ever possible to separate subject (the knower) and object (the known) in the manner postulated by positivism. Simply put, if the paradigm (language game/tradition/discourse) tells us not only how to interpret evidence, but determines what will count as valid evidence in the first place, the tenet of 'truth as correspondence' to 'the facts' can no longer be sustained.

Thus it is that the notion of reflexivity directs us beyond merely identifying the underlying assumptions of our theorizing. It directs us to recognize that the very existence of objective standards for assessing competing knowledge claims must be questioned. It moves us to understand that the standards which determine what is to count as reliable knowledge are not nature's, but rather always *human* standards – standards which are not given but made, not imposed by nature but adopted by convention by the members of a specific community.

In so doing, moreover, we are compelled to acknowledge the politico-normative content of scholarly investigation. Seeing knowledge-defining standards as community-created conventions in specific contexts moves us to see that

> evolving descriptions and ever-changing versions of objects, things, and the world issue forth from various communities as *responses to certain problems, as attempts to overcome specific situations, and as means to satisfy particular needs and interests.*[9]

In short, 'ideas, words, and language are not mirrors which copy the "real" or "objective" world' – as positivist conceptions of theory and knowledge would have it – 'but rather tools with which we cope with "our" world'.[10] Consequently, there is a fundamental link between epistemology – the question of what counts as 'reliable knowledge' – and politics: the problems, needs and interests deemed important and legitimate by a given community for which 'reliable knowledge' is being sought.[11]

The inextricably politico-normative aspect of scholarship has an important consequence for the social sciences in terms of the incommensurability thesis (that contending paradigms are not only incompatible but actually have 'no common measure'). In the case of the natural sciences, one may reasonably contest the thesis that contending paradigms are incommensurable, given their shared politico-normative goal of instrumental control of nature.[12] In the case of the social sciences, however, different paradigms have not only different terminologies, but are often constructed in terms of quite different values and oriented to serving quite different political projects. Consequently, the thesis of the radical incommensurability of contending paradigms in a social science such as International Relations is much more difficult to dispute.[13]

We arrive now at the third element of a fully reflexive orientation: the affirmation of the possibility of reasoned judgments in the absence of objective standards. Once again, this element of reflexivity can best be understood in relation to positivism. As was noted above, positivism strives, by means of the separation of subject and object, to derive a 'neutral observation language' which will allow for a point by point comparison of rival paradigms. In this context, it is important to note the possibility of a reasoned assessment of empirical

43

claims. Indeed, it is not going too far to assert that for positivists this assumption is at the core of reason itself.

The faith in the possibility of a neutral observation language and the accompanying conviction that such a language is a necessary condition for reasoned assessment explains much of the distress exhibited by positivists in the face of the assertions about incommensurability. To accept incommensurability is, for positivists, to promote what Popper termed the 'Myth of the Framework' according to which 'we are prisoners caught in the framework of our theories; our expectations; our past experiences; our language', and that as a consequence we cannot communicate with or judge those working in terms of a different paradigm.[14]

In contrast, reflexive theorists accept incommensurability as the necessary consequence of the fact that paradigm-specific knowledge-defining standards are themselves intimately connected to and embedded in competing social and political agendas, the politico-normative contents of which are not amenable to any neutral observation language.[15] At the same time, however, reflexive theorists do not accept that recognizing contending paradigms as incommensurable means reasoned assessments are impossible. Rather, a reflexive orientation sees how both the positivist insistence on 'truth as correspondence' and Popper's notion of the 'Myth of the Framework' are expressions of a common philosophical apprehension. They are both expressions of what Bernstein has termed the 'Cartesian anxiety' – the notion, central to identitarian thinking from René Descartes to the present, that should we prove unsuccessful in our search for the Archimedean point of indubitable knowledge which can serve as the foundation for human reason, then rationality must give way to irrationality, and reliable knowledge to madness.[16]

As the driving force of modern philosophy, the Cartesian anxiety – which is reflected in positivism's insistence on the ahistorical, extra-social standard of 'truth as correspondence' – is bound up with the conception of knowledge that Aristotle called *episteme*: apodictic knowledge of the order and nature of the cosmos. Furthermore, the peculiarly modern fear that the undermining of the viability of *episteme* must lead inexorably to irrationality and chaos is the result of the limiting of the modern conception of knowledge and rationality to *episteme*.

It is this limiting of reason, moreover, which has resulted in the marginalization and impoverishment of normative discourse. Given the positivist emphasis on the centrality of a neutral observation language, the treatment of normative issues in mainstream social science has typically taken the form of descriptive accounts of individual value preferences. One might, of course, engage in crude utilitarian calculation to determine the course offering the most in terms of human happiness. Foreclosed, however, is the reasoned adjudication of the inherent value of competing normative claims. Indeed, in the realm of normative discourse the hold of the positivist model of social science has been so powerful that it has made us 'quite incapable of seeing how reason does and can really function in the domain'.[17]

Consequently, the means of exorcising the Cartesian anxiety lies in elucidating a conception of reason which is not limited to *episteme*, and which does not depend on a fixed Archimedean point outside of history or on the existence of a neutral observation language. It is worth noting that just such an effort has been underway in contemporary social and political theory. It is evident in Charles Taylor's privileging of Hegel's 'interpretive or hermeneutical dialectics' – a form of reasoning which, in contrast to the claim of 'strict dialectics' (which makes claims to an undeniable starting point), posits no such foundation and yet still aims to convince us by means of reasoned arguments: 'by the overall plausibility of the interpretations [it] give[s]'.[18] It is evident in Hans-Georg Gadamer's linguistically based reappropriation of the Aristotelian notion of *phronesis* which, in contrast to *episteme*, is oriented to the exercise of reasoned judgment not in the context of the timeless and unchanging, but of the variable and contingent.[19] It is evident in Jürgen Habermas' contribution to the theory of 'communicative action', in particular the discursive validation of truth claims.[20] And perhaps most strikingly, given the predominance achieved by the notion of 'paradigm' in contemporary International Relations theory, it is evident in Richard Bernstein's re-evaluation of Kuhn, as someone whose work leads us not to the Myth of the Framework – as was charged by Popper – but rather evidences a movement toward a form of 'practical reason' having great affinity to Gadamer's reconceptualization of *phronesis*.[21] In all of these efforts and more, the emphasis is upon the elucidation of a form of reason which refuses to limit our conception of human rationality to a mechanical application of an eternal, unchanging standard; which affirms that a broader and more subtle conception of reason is possible than that which underlies both the positivist tenet

45

of 'truth as correspondence' and that of radical relativism as the logical consequence of incommensurability; which experiences no self-contradiction when employing a 'language of qualitative worth', and which is thus as suited to a consideration of normative claims as it is to empirical ones.

Expanding the conception of reason beyond positivistic *episteme* is vital to a reflexive orientation. For having reclaimed normative discourse as a domain in which reason can and does function, reflexive theorists argue that what makes paradigms incommensurable – the politico-normative content of the normal science they generate – also makes reasoned assessments of them possible. In short, judgments about contending paradigms are possible by means of reasoned assessments of the politico-normative content of the projects they serve, of the ways of life to which they correspond.[22]

Having established what reflexivity is, perhaps it would be useful, by way of conclusion, to state briefly what it is not. Reflexivity is not a 'research programme' designed to provide cumulative knowledge about the world of empirical facts or about the world of theory. Nor can reflexivity be reduced to the idea that while agreement on facts is possible, value disagreements will continue to plague scholars in their quest for disciplinary consensus. Finally, reflexivity does not provide specific, *a priori* standards or criteria for assessing the merits of contending paradigms.

Reflexivity is 'theoretical self-consciousness' involving (i) a recognition of the interrelationship of the conception of 'facts' and 'values' on the one hand, and a community-specific social and political agenda on the other, and (ii) an openness to engaging in reasoned dialogue to assess the merits of contending paradigms. Whether this kind of self-consciousness is in evidence in recent theorizing within the discipline of International Relations is the question we shall now address.

Reflexivity and International Relations theory

We move now to a consideration of reflexivity in terms of International Relations theory. I will begin by examining a recent meta-theoretical debate in the discipline: International Relations theory's 'Third Debate'. Specifically, I will examine the contributions of a sampling of International Relations scholars to the Third Debate to determine to what extent the elements of reflexivity are in evidence. I

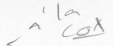

will argue that in terms of the Third Debate, the break with positivist conceptions of theory and knowledge is, at best, partial and that the contribution of the Third Debate to reflexivity is, consequently, a limited one.

The focus will then be shifted to the contributions of scholars representing three minority traditions in the discipline: (i) neo-Gramscian International Relations theory; (ii) postmodern International Relations theory; and (iii) feminist International Relations theory. I will argue that it is here, at the 'margins' of the discipline, that the best evidence is to be found – and the best hopes reside – for a truly 'reflexive turn' in International Relations.

The Third Debate reconsidered

International Relations theory's Third Debate, which dates from the late 1980s, can be seen as the third in a series of 'discipline-defining' debates[23] in the twentieth century: the first being that between 'idealism' and 'realism' in the 1940s and 1950s,[24] with the second, which occurred during the 1960s, centring around the confrontation between 'history' and 'science'.[25]

On the one hand, one can understand the Third Debate in the same general terms as the First and Second: namely, as an expression of the on-going quest for better theory. At the same time, one should also see the Third Debate in terms of contemporary developments in the realm of social and political theory more generally. It has already been suggested in this study that the claim that 'International Relations is a discrete area of action and discourse, separate from social and political theory',[26] can no longer be sustained. In fact, nowhere is there better evidence for this position than in International Relations theory's Third Debate.

To reiterate, like the debates which preceded it, the Third Debate is part of the search for better theory. In the case of the Third Debate, however, and in line with current social and political theory, this search is being conducted not in terms of individual propositions or hypotheses, but in terms of larger conceptual schemes. The Third Debate is a 'discourse about choice of analytic frameworks'.[27] It involves a focus on 'meta-scientific units' (i.e., paradigms), where particular attention is directed to examining the 'underlying premises and assumptions' of the paradigms in contention.[28]

A good example of this approach to the on-going quest for better theory is the work of Michael Banks. In an important contribution to the Third Debate, Banks conceptualizes the present state of the discipline in terms of three contending paradigms: realism, pluralism, and structuralism. 'The debate about their respective merits', argues Banks, 'occupies centre stage in the discipline'.[29]

Banks attempts to detail and contrast the 'basic images' of the respective paradigms. He notes:

> Each of the three starts with a wholly different basic image. For realists, the world society is a system of 'billiard-ball' states in intermittent collision. For pluralists, it is a 'cobweb', a network of numerous criss-crossing relationships. For structuralists, it is a 'multi-headed octopus', with powerful tentacles constantly sucking wealth from the weakened peripheries towards the powerful centres.[30]

It is these contrasting images, notes Banks, that serve as the foundation for the erection of theoretical structures. These structures, while internally coherent, contradict one another in terms of major theoretical categories including (i) actors, (ii) dynamics, (iii) dependent variables, (iv) subject boundaries, and (v) specific concepts.

With regard to actors, writes Banks, 'realists see only states; pluralists see states in combination with a great variety of others; and structuralists see classes'. As regards dynamics, 'realists see force as primary; pluralists see complex social movements; structuralists see economics'. As concerns dependent variables,

> realists see the task of IR [International Relations] as simply to explain what states do; pluralists see it more grandly as an effort to explain all major world events; and structuralists see its function as showing why the world contains such appalling contrasts between rich and poor.[31]

With regard to subject boundaries,

> Realists define the boundaries of their subject in a narrow, state-centric fashion, often preferring the term 'international politics' to describe it. Pluralists widen the boundaries by including multi-national companies, markets, ethnic groups and nationalism as well as state behaviour, and call their subject IR or world society. Structuralists have the widest boundaries of all, stressing the unity of the whole world system at all levels, focusing on modes of production and treating inter-state politics as merely a surface phenomenon.[32]

And finally, as regards specific concepts, Banks notes that:

> Some concepts are found only in one paradigm, because they are of crucial importance to it: deterrence and alliances in realism, ethnicity and interdependence in pluralism, exploitation and dependency in structuralism. Others, however, are used with broadly similar meanings in all three: power, sovereignty, and law, for example. Yet others, like imperialism, the state, and hegemony, are used in all three but with sharply different interpretations.[33]

It is clear there is much room for disagreement with the specifics of Banks' intervention. His conceptualization of the contending paradigms – from their basic images through to their contrasting notions of actors, dynamics, etc. – can be challenged as to its accuracy and adequacy. Indeed, disagreements may extend all the way to the labels used to designate contending paradigms.[34] In contrast to Banks' use of the terms 'realism', 'pluralism', and 'structuralism', for example, Kal Holsti prefers those of the 'Classical Tradition', 'Global Society', and 'Neo-Marxism';[35] Paul Viotti and Mark Kauppi employ those of 'realism', 'pluralism', and 'globalism';[36] R. D. McKinlay and R. Little identify their paradigms by the labels of 'realist', 'liberal', and 'socialist'.[37] The point remains, however, that Banks' work serves as an excellent example of how the emphases of contemporary philosophy of science have spilled over into International Relations, and influenced the form that interventions have taken in the Third Debate.

As was noted above, the Third Debate, like its forerunners, is a discipline-defining debate, concerned with the 'search for better theory'.[38] For that reason alone, it bears consideration. However, the Third Debate has special significance in terms of the concerns of the present chapter. For beyond the immediate arguments about the number, identifying characteristics, and appropriate labels for the paradigms in International Relations theory, the Third Debate affords a valuable opportunity for exploring the issue of theoretical reflexivity in the discipline.

It has been argued that International Relations theory's Third Debate not only reflects the influence of contemporary philosophy of science in general (with its emphasis on meta-scientific units), but that it is a direct expression of *post/anti-positivist* currents. In the words of Yosef Lapid, the Third Debate is 'linked, historically and intellectually, to the confluence of diverse anti-positivistic philosophical and sociological trends'.[39] Indeed, it is because the Third Debate has been understood as marking International Relations theory's break with positivist orthodoxy that it has been associated with an important increase in theoretical reflexivity within International Relations.[40]

In the pages which follow, this interpretation of the Third Debate will be examined. It will be argued that to see the Third Debate as marking a conclusive break with the positivist legacy, and an opening to theoretical reflexivity, would be a mistake. Rather, it will be suggested that for two important reasons, the Third Debate's contribution to increased reflexivity in the discipline has been limited. First, a significant number of interventions in the Third Debate continue to be structured in terms of positivism's tenet of 'truth as correspondence'. And secondly, of the interventions which do evidence an attempt to break with the notion of 'truth as correspondence', the vast majority remain trapped within positivist-derived conceptions of reasoned assessment. In both cases, reflexivity remains foreclosed.

Interventions in the Third Debate

On the basis of our discussion of positivism and reflexivity in the first part of this chapter, three possible stances with regard to contending paradigms can be distinguished.[41] The first stance, having its basis in the acceptance of the positivist tenet of 'truth as correspondence', is that of 'commensurable and therefore comparable'. Rival paradigms are comparable, asserts this position, because ultimately they can be assessed according to a common standard – that of correspondence to the real world. This stance, it will be remembered, is incompatible with the development of theoretical reflexivity, in that it sees the standard for what constitutes reliable knowledge as 'Nature's own', and thus beyond criticism.

A second stance with regard to contending paradigms is that which corresponds to the Popperian notion of the 'Myth of the Framework'. According to this stance, rival paradigms are 'incommensurable and therefore incomparable'. This stance breaks with positivism to the degree that it recognizes that standards for what constitutes reliable knowledge are human constructs and social conventions. However, it remains firmly attached to the positivist conception of reasoned assessment – in particular, the idea that the acceptance of incommensurability means that rival standards cannot be compared and assessed. While embodying the first two elements of reflexivity, then, this stance nonetheless fails in relation to the third.

Finally, a third stance can be identified. According to this stance – a stance associated with efforts to elucidate dialogic, non-foundationalist conceptions of reason – rival paradigms are 'incommensurable yet still comparable'. This stance recognizes the social and political nature of the standards for what constitutes 'reliable knowledge', of the 'coping vocabularies' devised by different communities. But it also affirms that these conventions and vocabularies can be compared and assessed by means of reasoned argument and deliberation about their politico-normative content. It is this stance – and this stance alone – which qualifies as fully reflexive.

With these three stances in mind, we can now move to an examination of the Third Debate. Interventions in the Third Debate can be classified and assessed in terms of their break with positivism and their contribution to reflexivity. We will begin with the first stance: that of 'commensurable and therefore comparable'.

Stance I: commensurable and therefore comparable

One of the best examples of 'Stance I' in the Third Debate is to be found in the writings of K. J. Holsti.[42] To begin, there is no question that Holsti is most comfortable within the realist – or in his terms, 'Classical' – tradition. Indeed, *The Dividing Discipline* can be seen as a spirited defence of the realist approach to the study of international politics at a time when calls are being heard for its replacement.

What is even more important in terms of the present discussion, however, is Holsti's adherence to a (Lakatosian) version of positivism, and his consequent acceptance of the positivist tenet of 'truth as correspondence'. Holsti's allegiance to positivism is clearly evidenced in his statements concerning the purpose of theory and the nature of knowledge accumulation. For Holsti, 'the ultimate purpose of theoretical activity is to enhance our understanding of the world of international politics'; it is to 'increase our knowledge of the *real world* by helping to guide research and interpret data'.[43] Moreover, notes Holsti, 'We add to knowledge primarily when we render reality more intelligible by seeking generalizations of empirical validity ... '[44]

It is out of the understanding that theory is a reflection of the 'real world' that Holsti explains the origins of the contending paradigms which constitute the Third Debate. 'A plethora of ... "paradigms"', notes Holsti, 'is an expression of greater international complexity'.[45] And because '[o]ur world is complex and growing more so', he asserts, 'it is ... unlikely that any single theory or perspective ... could adequately explain all of its essential characteristics'.[46] Thus, he concludes, 'Theoretical pluralism is the only possible response to the multiple realities of a complex world.'[47]

It should be noted, however, that for Holsti, paradigmatic pluralism is more than just an inevitable condition of theorizing which tries to comprehend a complex reality. In addition, pluralism is an important principle which, when respected, serves some very beneficial functions. Clearly echoing Lakatos' rejection of the Popperian notion of strict falsification, Holsti affirms that:

> Pluralism ... guards against the hazards of 'intellectual knockouts', those attempts to disown past methodologies and theories on the assumption that they are entirely wrong ... This was a major shortcoming of the most extreme behaviorism and of some recent efforts to demolish realism and its variants.[48]

In addition to guarding against straightforward falsification of paradigms which, despite anomalies, have proven their worth as interpretive tools, the principle of pluralism also serves to ensure that the discipline keeps progressing in its quest for ever truer descriptions of reality. Thus, notes Holsti, if the dominant realist tradition shows itself to be inadequate as a description of reality, 'then new departures may help us redirect inquiry into the proper channels'. If realism is lacking, argues Holsti, it can be refurbished by 'grafting' new theoretical formulations on to it.[49]

It is important to note that despite his support for paradigmatic pluralism, Holsti is not arguing that all paradigms are of equal value. In keeping with the positivist tenet of 'truth as correspondence', paradigms may be evaluated according to the accuracy of their description of the facts. Notes Holsti,

> Progress is thus not measured by unlimited accumulation of perspectives, paradigms, models, or methodologies any more than it is by the replacement of 'units of knowledge'. Some perspectives, models, and the like should and do have higher intellectual claims than others. The ultimate test is how elegantly and comprehensibly they describe and explain the *important* persisting, new, and developing realities.[50]

Thus it is that early in *The Dividing Discipline*, Holsti affirms that 'isomorphism' and 'correspondence with the observed facts of international politics' are the standards by which rival paradigms must be assessed.[51]

Indeed, it is on the basis of its transhistorical correspondence with the facts that Holsti continues to promote the realist paradigm over its rivals. In an interesting reversal of the traditional sense of inferiority experienced by social scientists in regard to their counterparts in the natural sciences, Holsti affirms that:

> We cannot throw away paradigms (or what passes for them) as natural scientists do, á la Kuhn, because the anomalies between reality and its theoretical characterization are never so severe in International Relations as they are in the natural sciences. None of the thinkers of the past portrayed the world of international (or world) politics in so distorted a manner as did the analysts of the physical or astronomical universe prior to the Copernican revolution.[52]

From his affirmations that competing paradigms may be 'synthesized' ('grafted' one on to another), and that realists have been more successful than many physicists in approximating reality – not to mention his assertion that 'correspondence with the observed facts of international politics' is the basis upon which rival paradigms must be assessed – it is clear that Holsti does not accept the incommensurability thesis. The theory-ladenness of all facts, not to mention the politico-normative content of all theorizing, is something he cannot embrace. Notes Holsti,

> I remain sceptical of the 'liberation of theory from data', or as Halliday has put it, a 'rejection of empiricism in favor of a theoretical approach that accepts the place of data in a subordinate position'.[53]

The implications of Holsti's rejection of the notion of incommensurability for increased theoretical reflexivity are clear. In the continued affirmation of the notion that 'Nature's own' standards – specifically, 'truth as correspondence' – must be applied in the knowledge validation process, the possibility of critical reflection on the social origins and politico-normative content of the conventions which define what is to count as reliable knowledge remains remote. Theoretical reflexivity, to the degree that it figures at all, is reduced to the much more limited notion of 'careful examination of assumptions and premises' – a notion that Holsti correctly notes is perfectly consistent with positivism.[54]

In conclusion, it should be noted that the greater part of the interventions in the Third Debate – of which Holsti's stands out only because of his clarity – conform to the positivist-inspired stance of 'commensurable and therefore comparable'. As a consequence, the interpretation of the Third Debate as marking a disciplinary shift toward post-positivist theoretical reflexivity bears being reconsidered.

Stance II: incommensurable and therefore incomparable

Although the majority of the interventions in International Relations theory's Third Debate reflect what has been termed here 'Stance I',[55] it should be noted that there are important exceptions. Noteworthy among these are those theorists who have adopted the second stance: that of 'incommensurable and therefore incomparable'.

An important intervention by R. D. McKinlay and R. Little – *Global Problems and World Order* – is a good example of this stance in the Third Debate. McKinlay and Little's starting point is that the source of the paradigms found in the literature – in their terms, Realism, Liberalism, and Socialism – is not to be found in 'international complexity' (where paradigmatic pluralism is seen as the inevitable by-product). Rather, contending paradigms are expressions of radically different politico-normative orders embedded in competing ideological frameworks.

Highlighting the links between paradigms and specific social–political agendas is one of the ways in which Stance II adherents demonstrate a clear advance over those of Stance I in terms of reflexivity.[56] The treatment of the realist paradigm in International Relations theory serves as a good example. As Smith has argued, because International Relations theory, as primarily an 'American discipline', has been

> so closely identified with the foreign policy concerns of the country, it is not surprising that the assumptions of Realism have proven to be so difficult to overcome. This is because the focus of Realism, namely how to maximize power so as to manage international events, fits extraordinarily well with the needs of a hegemonic power. The three key elements of Realism's account of world politics, the national interest, power maximization and the balance of power, are particularly well-suited to the requirements of a foreign policy for the US.[57]

In short, from the perspective of Stance II, realism is understood not as a neutral description of the world as it 'truly is', but rather as a 'coping' vocabulary of a specific community (e.g., US state managers) designed to address certain problems, to satisfy particular needs and interests.

Furthermore, the assessment of realism as a 'coping' vocabulary can be undertaken only in relation to the problems defined, the needs and interests identified. Consequently, the success of realism has, *pace* Holsti, had less to do with its alleged accuracy in grasping the 'facts' of international politics, than with its demonstrated utility for guiding state managers in their activities of 'state- and nation-building'. That is to say, the realist paradigm has validated its truth-claims by demonstrating its ability to guide state policy-making;[58] realism is 'true' because it has met the needs of the policy-makers of the great powers – most recently and perhaps most importantly, the United States – engaged in the pursuit of a specific agenda and faced 'with a specific set of foreign policy problems'.[59]

If the success of the realist paradigm cannot be understood apart from particular social actors and their political projects – specifically US state managers dedicated to the maintenance of American hegemony – then a similar relationship must hold for other paradigms. Notes Smith,

> Just as it has been argued ... that the US policy agenda dominated the study of International Relations by dominating Realism within the US, so we should expect different paradigms [i.e. pluralism and structuralism] to appeal to persons in different settings.[60]

In their discussion of rival paradigms in International Relations theory, Alker and Biersteker adopt a similar tack. It is noteworthy that their stated aim is to evidence a 'broader and deeper kind of political and epistemological self-consciousness' than that found within the positivist tradition – a self-consciousness which recognizes 'the deep connections between the social and political contexts of particular theoretical enterprises and the kind of work actually done'.[61] Thus, in a manner similar to Smith, they affirm that:

> Two global superpowers both able to destroy each other, but likely to self-destruct in the same process, are likely to have scholars especially interested in 'global interdependence' or 'peaceful coexistence'. Anti-colonial revolutionaries in relatively undeveloped countries are driven by other practical imperatives.[62]

In sum, unlike Stance I, Stance II accepts that contending paradigms in International Relations theory are incommensurable, and that the hope held out by the adherents of Stance I – that of paradigm 'synthesis' – is thus a pipedream. The consequence of incommensurability, note McKinlay and Little, is that

> even when the models [i.e. paradigms] look to the same topics, the general framework within which the topic is processed leads to systematic variation in problem explication.[63]

As a consequence, 'as any one model begins to engineer solutions to its perceived problems, it will in all likelihood create a problem for another model'.[64]

With their rejection of the notion of a theory-independent realm of facts by which one can assess the merits of competing paradigms, and a recognition of the politico-normative content of the normal science traditions, adherents of Stance II appear to be on the post-positivist path to theoretical reflexivity. Unfortunately, this is not the case. It is not the case because the adherents of Stance II remain trapped by a notion of reason limited to *episteme*. Consequently, they equate the incommensurability of paradigms with the incomparability of paradigms.

Again, McKinlay and Little serve as a useful example. The ability to assess the merits of competing paradigms, they argue, 'presupposes some form of comparatively valid evaluation procedure, entailing some decision rule which would stipulate which model was to be retained'. And since any evaluation procedure which might be proposed would be no more than a social convention, and hence, inherently contestable, comparative assessments are virtually impossible. The 'only comparatively valid test procedure', they conclude, 'is to inquire whether each model is internally consistent'.[65] And this criterion they judge to be met in each case.

Indeed, not only is comparative assessment virtually impossible, argue McKinlay and Little, but the very idea of meaningful communication between the adherents of rival paradigms – and the learning which is a product of that communication – is out of the question:

> [The] sophistication and internal coherence of each model, combined with their very different goals, structural arrangements and belief systems, make meaningful inter-model debate well-nigh impossible ... Compromise and constructive debate can largely only be conducted within the confines and parameters of a single model.[66]

Given this view of incommensurability, the comparative assessment of the substantive content of rival paradigms is foreclosed completely. Relating rival paradigms one to another is possible only by means of a 'sociology of knowledge', that is, a discussion of the social origins and purposes of the paradigms in question. Yet as Adorno noted, the problem with the sociology of knowledge is that it is inherently relativistic – it involves no reasoned assessment of the merits of the knowledge systems being investigated.[67]

Given the assumption of the essential incomparability of paradigms, how is one to account for paradigm choice by members of the research community? The position of James Rosenau on this issue is a good example of how Stance II adherents respond to this question. In accordance with the core assumptions of the stance of 'incommensurable and therefore incomparable', Rosenau affirms that 'the way in which analysts become adherents of one or another approach is not necessarily based on intellectual or rational calculation'. What then is the explanation for paradigm choice? By definition, the explanation must be found outside the realm of reason and argumentation. Rosenau's answer is consistent, if disconcerting: 'our temperaments', he affirms, '... are the central determinants of which approach we will find most suitable'.[68]

To conclude then, the second stance of 'incommensurable and therefore incomparable',[69] while having broken with positivism in important respects, remains trapped within the positivist-reinforced limitation of reason to *episteme*. Neither reasoned assessment nor even communication between paradigms is possible. By definition, they are condemned to 'pass like ships in the night'.[70] As a consequence, and despite some important progress beyond Stance I, for Stance II reflexivity remains foreclosed.

Beyond the Third Debate

We have examined the two stances to which the interventions in mainstream International Relations theory's Third Debate correspond. In each case, we have seen that the possibilities for the development of theoretical reflexivity – to the degree that they exist at all – remain limited. At the same time, the third stance of 'incommensurable yet still comparable', the only stance which represents a fully reflexive orientation, is not represented. This raises an important question: beyond the Third Debate, is there any evidence of this third stance in contemporary theorizing in the discipline?

For examples of this third stance it is necessary to move outside of the mainstream to the margins of the discipline. Here three distinct efforts will be examined: (i) Gramscian-inspired neo-Marxist International Relations theory; (ii) postmodern International Relations theory, and (iii) feminist International Relations theory.

The first tradition is that of the Gramscian-inspired neo-Marxist International Relations theory represented by Robert Cox. In a piece which predates the Third Debate by several years, Cox evidences a clear awareness of the core elements of theoretical reflexivity. Beyond attention to basic assumptions, Cox also shows awareness of the politico-normative content of any theoretical enterprise. Specifically, he argues that it is necessary to recognize that 'Theory is always *for* someone and *for* some purpose'; that theory is shaped by a problematic rooted in the 'human experience that gives rise to the need for theory'.[71] Accordingly, there is 'no such thing as theory in itself, divorced from a standpoint in time and space'. As a consequence, argues Cox, 'When any theory so represents itself, it is more important to examine it as ideology, and to lay bare its concealed perspective.'[72]

In short, paradigms/theories are expressions of diverse perspectives linked to disparate social and political projects. It is, therefore, a central task of the theorist to achieve 'a perspective on perspectives' by becoming 'more reflective upon the process of theorizing itself'; by becoming 'clearly aware of the perspective which gives rise to theorizing, and its relation to other perspectives'.[73]

As such, Cox's position represents a clear break with the positivist notion of truth as correspondence and distinguishes itself clearly from the stance of 'commensurable and therefore comparable'. At the same time, it is important to note that Cox breaks as well with the position of Stance II. Refusing to equate incommensurability with incomparability, Cox affirms that achieving a 'perspective on perspectives' is oriented to a specific goal: 'to open up the possibility of *choosing a different valid perspective*'.[74]

The perspective on perspectives which Cox presents involves a distinction between two types of theorizing – two distinct, rival and incommensurable paradigms. The first Cox labels 'problem-solving theory', an approach distinguished by the fact that it takes the world as it finds it, with the prevailing social and power relationships and the institutions into which they are organized, as the given framework for action.[75]

In contrast to 'problem-solving' theory, the second approach – that of 'critical theory' – is distinguished by the fact that it 'stands apart from the prevailing order of the world and asks how that order came about'; that it 'does not take institutions and social and power relations for granted but calls them into question by concerning itself with their origins and how and whether they might be in the process of changing'.[76]

Despite the recognition of the incommensurability of these two approaches, Cox shows himself quite ready to engage in a reasoned comparison of them by means of a critical examination of their politico-normative contents. Notes Cox:

> The strength of the problem-solving approach lies in its ability to fix limits or parameters to a problem area and to reduce the statement of a particular problem to a limited number of variables which are amenable to relatively close and precise examination. The *ceteris paribus* assumption, upon which such theorizing is based, makes it possible to arrive at statements of laws or regularities which appear to have general validity but which imply, of course, the institutional and relational parameters assumed in the problem-solving approach.[77]

However, Cox insists, problem-solving theory's assumption of a fixed order

> is not merely a convenience of method, but also an ideological bias. Problem-solving theories can be represented ... as serving particular national, sectional, or class interests, which are comfortable within the given order. Indeed, the purpose served by problem-solving theory is conservative, since it aims to solve the problems arising in various parts of a complex whole in order to smooth the functioning of the whole.[78]

In contrast to problem-solving theory, critical theory recognizes that it stems from a perspective. Secondly, 'critical theory contains problem-solving theories within itself, but contains them in the form of identifiable ideologies, thereby pointing to their conservative consequences'.[79] And thirdly, critical theory having as a 'principal objective' the clarification of the 'range of possible alternatives', 'allows for a normative choice in favour of a social and political order different from the prevailing order'.[80] Thus, while acknowledging problem-solving theory's strengths,[81] Cox nonetheless judges 'critical theory' superior on the basis of its emancipatory politico-normative content.

Now it is of course possible to raise reasoned objections to Cox's conclusion regarding the relative merits of the two approaches. But the contestability of his conclusions should not distract us from the main contribution of Cox's intervention in terms of reflexivity: namely that reasoned comparison of incommensurable approaches is not only necessary but possible, and that it is possible once one extends the grounds of assessment to include the politico-normative dimensions of rival theoretical enterprises.

Despite the importance of Cox's contribution, however, it must be conceded that his intervention remains preliminary and in need of further development. In this regard, it is hopeful to note that Cox's concern with promoting a reflexive brand of theorizing is being taken up by others within the tradition of Gramscian-inspired analysis of world politics.[82] Yet it can be argued that it is within non-Gramscian theoretical traditions – those of postmodern International Relations and feminist International Relations – that the notions that theory is always 'for something' and 'for someone' have been taken up most intensively.

At first glance, the potential for postmodern International Relations theory to contribute to reflexivity would seem quite good. To begin, postmodern approaches recognize the highly problematic nature of the positivist tenet of 'truth as correspondence', arguing that the world is never known except through a 'discourse' which 'generates the categories of meaning by which reality can be understood and explained' and which 'makes "real" that which *it* prescribes as meaningful'.[83]

It is with regard to the insight that all theory has politico-normative content, however, that postmodernism makes its main contribution to reflexivity. As George has noted, the distinguishing characteristic of postmodernism is that it 'refocuses contemporary analysis on the power/knowledge nexus and ... on theory *as* practice'.[84] Accordingly, drawing out the hidden politico-normative content of ostensibly neutral, apolitical knowledge–discourses has been a major focus of postmodern theorizing more generally.[85] This concern is clearly in evidence in the work of postmodern International Relations scholars, who have insisted that all theorizing about world politics is done from some perspective, and that the goal of 'apocalyptic objectivity' – that is, 'a totalizing standpoint outside of time and capable of enclosing all history within a singular narrative, a law of development, or a vision of progress toward a certain end of humankind'[86] – is untenable.

It is in their specific attentiveness to the politico-normative content of mainstream International Relations theorizing that postmodernist theorists have distinguished themselves.[87] Their contributions in this regard include (i) showing standard interpretations of Machiavelli as a proto-realist to be reflective of a contemporary quest to legitimize the practices of *Realpolitik*;[88] (ii) demonstrating the link between the 'great texts' of diplomatic discourse, the social context of which it was both an expression and shaper, and the designation by that discourse of which practices would be viewed as legitimate and which not;[89] and (iii) exploring the crucial role of contemporary 'strategy/security discourse' in providing justification for realist practice and constraining non-traditional conceptualizations of security.[90] In these ways and more, postmodern International Relations theorists have reinforced the reflexive insight that theory is always 'for something'.

At the same time it must be acknowledged that aspects of postmodern International Relations raise serious questions as to its potential to contribute to increased reflexivity. A central difficulty lies in the ambiguous relationship of postmodernist theorizing to reason and, by extension, to reasoned critique. Postmodernism more generally has been faulted for equating instrumental rationality with reason *tout court*[91] – an equation which, if taken to its logical endpoint, entails a rejection not only of domination rooted in instrumental reason, but a rejection of reasoned criticism itself. As Bernstein notes in reference to Foucault's work:

> Critique – even genealogical critique – must preserve at least one standard by which we engage in the critique of the present. Yet when critique is *totalized*, when critique turns against itself so that all rational standards are called into question, then one is caught in a performative contradiction.[92]

It is, of course, true that postmodernist theorists like Foucault have tried to distance themselves from the charge of irrationalism:

> There is the problem raised by Habermas: if one abandons the work of Kant or Weber, for example, one runs the risk of lapsing into irrationality.

61

> I am completely in agreement with this, but at the same time, our
> question is quite different: I think that the central issue of philosophy
> and critical thought since the eighteenth century has always been,
> still is, and will, I hope, remain the question, *What* is this reason that
> we use? What are its historical effects? What are its limits, and what
> are its dangers? How can we exist as rational beings, fortunately
> committed to practicing a rationality unfortunately crisscrossed by
> intrinsic dangers? ... In addition, if it is extremely dangerous to say
> that Reason is the enemy that should be eliminated, it is just as
> dangerous to say that any critical questioning of this rationality risks
> sending us into irrationality.[93]

This disclaimer notwithstanding, however, what remains lacking in
Foucault's work 'is an attempt to discriminate among aspects (or
versions) of rationality in order to locate more clearly its beneficial
and pernicious dimensions'.[94] The difficulty this poses for reflexivity
is clear, given the centrality of the notion that reasoned judgments are
possible even in the face of incommensurability.

The ambiguous status of reason in postmodernism generally is
paralleled by a similarly ambiguous status within postmodern International Relations theory. Indeed, the conclusion that postmodern
International Relations harbours an underlying current of 'irrationalism' has become commonplace in the writings of the critics of
postmodern International Relations.[95] And as in the case of Foucault,
it has become equally commonplace for postmodern International
Relations theorists to attempt to repudiate this charge. What they
reject is not reason, argue postmodern International Relations theorists, but rather a conception of reason which remains entrapped
within Bernstein's notion of the 'Cartesian anxiety' – 'the modernist
proposition which asserts that either we have some sort of ultimate
'foundation' for our knowledge or we are plunged into the void of
the relative, the irrational, the arbitrary, the nihilistic'.[96] In a similar
vein, Ashley and Walker's defence of a postmodern 'ethics of
freedom' against the charge that it sanctions 'a sort of licentious
activity whose credo might be "Anything goes!"'[97] can be read as an
affirmation of the possibility of the reasoned adjudication of rival
politico-normative claims which is central to comparing the incommensurable. When words and deeds proceed in the 'register of
freedom', they argue, this does not mean that

> every notion of criticizing and disciplining conduct is out the
> window because, given the refusal to refer conduct to some

presumably fixed and universal standard of judgment, every word and deed must be presumed to be as good, as ethical, or as effective as the next.[98]

At the same time, it must also be acknowledged that certain interventions by postmodern International Relations theorists do raise questions about the conception of reason which informs postmodern theorizing. Let us take, for example, Ashley's affirmation that

> Poststructuralism [postmodernism] cannot claim to offer an alternative position or perspective, *because there is no alternative ground upon which it might be established*.[99]

In denying the existence of objective grounds on which to privilege one perspective over another, Ashley is clearly breaking with the positivist–empiricist stance of 'commensurable and therefore comparable'. However, in twinning the rejection of foundational knowledge with the denial of the possibility of offering a reasoned defence of one politico-theoretical alternative over another, Ashley's affirmation remains captive to the logic of the 'Cartesian anxiety'. As such, postmodern International Relations would seem to offer no real challenge to positivism's limiting of reason to *episteme*.

Similarly, Rengger's critique of the critical conception of International Relations theory inspired by Cox, as presented by Mark Hoffman,[100] reproduces the terms of the 'Cartesian anxiety' in fairly standard terms. Rengger faults 'Coxian Critical Theory' for its explicit call for the creation of alternative orders better suited to promoting human welfare. The problem with such a call, he argues, is that it flies in the face of the 'thesis of radical value incommensurability' as developed in the works of postmodernists such as Foucault and Rorty.[101] His conclusion is not an unfamiliar one: critical theory's desire to mount a reasoned defence of an alternative order is proof that it remains 'foundationalist',[102] since it is only by achieving the 'view from nowhere'[103] that rational judgments about the incommensurable are possible.

It is true, of course, that foundationalist elements are identifiable in the work of individual critical International Relations theorists.[104] Yet it must also be recognized that in terms of reflexivity, Rengger's critique entails some rather problematic formulations of its own – particularly as regards his equating of incommensurability with incomparability, and his limiting of reason to *episteme*. As has already been noted, such formulations are quite consistent with positivist conceptions of reason, and, consequently, hardly compatible with a reflexive orientation.

It could, of course, be countered that these interventions by Ashley and Rengger are unrepresentative of postmodern International Relations more generally; alternatively, it might be suggested that this discussion simply misunderstands their arguments and the postmodern assumptions that inform them. Even so, Jay's critique of Foucault applies equally in this case. In the absence of a sustained effort by postmodern International Relations theorists to elucidate conceptions of reason and of reasoned criticism which would allow us to discriminate between the positive as well as the negative dimensions of rationality, it will remain difficult to counter the suspicion that postmodernist International Relations is better suited to undermining the role of reason *in toto* than to expanding the notion of reason beyond the confines of positivist *episteme* in a way consistent with reflexivity.

The final tradition to be considered is that of feminist International Relations theory. Here again, it can be argued that the contribution of feminist International Relations in terms of reflexivity is mixed. The main impediment to reflexivity within feminist International Relations is the presence of research agendas which are very much in keeping with the positivist logic of investigation. Termed 'feminist empiricism',[105] this orientation accepts the positivist assumption of the separation of subject and object/knower and known, and argues that 'sexism and androcentrism are identifiable biases of individual knowers that can be eliminated by stricter application of existing methodological norms of scientific and philosophical inquiry'.[106]

On the plus side, however, is the growing number of feminist theorists who are quite explicit in their rejection of the positivist tenet of 'truth as correspondence'. Notwithstanding the acceptance of positivist strictures by some feminists, Peterson argues convincingly that it has been one of the central contributions of feminist theory to problematize positivist notions of knowledge creation and validation. This strand of 'post-positivist' feminist International Relations advocates a theoretical self-consciousness involving the

> rejection of *transcendental* (decontextualized) criteria for assessing epistemological, ontological and/or normative claims and therefore the *necessity* of taking responsibility for the world(s) we make – including the criteria we construct for assessing epistemological, ontological, and normative claims.[107]

Like others who have rejected the regulative ideal of 'truth as correspondence', post-positivist feminists theorize 'the interdependence of categories and frameworks' in their efforts to 'expose the gender *politics* of categorizing practices'.[108] Equally significant in terms of reflexivity, however, is the recognition by feminist scholars that an advocacy of 'post-positivism' is not to be equated with the notion that there exists no possibility for a reasoned assessment of incommensurable frameworks.

In this regard it is worth noting recent interventions by post-positivist feminists on the question of which of the possible non-positivist epistemological orientations – 'feminist standpoint', 'feminist postmodernism', and 'critical feminism' – is best suited to the project of overcoming 'International Relations of gender inequality'.[109] It is significant that these interventions have been carried out without either recourse to positivist arguments about which approach better 'fits the facts' or by abandoning the issue of paradigm choice to the a(nti-)rational realm. Rather, post-positivist feminist International Relations theorists have endeavoured to draw out the politico-normative content of contending perspectives and frameworks – particularly in relation to the issue of *whom* theorizing is for – and have made that content a central focus in assessing the merits of contending epistemological orientations.

Runyan and Peterson's treatment of 'feminist standpoint' epistemologies is exemplary, and very much in keeping with a reflexive orientation's attentiveness to the politico-normative content of competing paradigms. Feminist standpoint epistemologies, typically associated with radical, cultural and socialist feminists, are grounded in 'historical materialism's insight that social being determines consciousness' and

> reject the notion of an 'unmediated truth', arguing that knowledge is always mediated by a host of factors related to an individual's particular position in a determinate sociopolitical formation at a specific point in history ... they argue that while certain social positions (the oppressor's) produce distorted ideological views of reality, other social positions (the oppressed's) can pierce ideological obfuscations.[110]

In Runyan and Peterson's view, what makes the standpoint solution attractive in the search for a systematized post-positivist epistemological framework is that it provides a basis for a feminist critique of androcentrism that feminist empiricism ends up forfeiting by its marriage to liberal positivism ... it offers an account of an 'alternative' and valorized gynocentric reality that seeks to significantly alter and, indeed, eradicate oppressive power relations at all levels in the world.[111]

They are equally concerned with feminist standpoint's politico-normative liabilities, however:

What is particularly troubling about the standpoint 'solution' ... is its *tendency* toward a dualistic treatment of gender, a monistic view of women, and an unsubstantiated faith in women's access to higher truth. In its quite justifiable urgency to undermine patriarchal discourse and practices, standpoint theory ... tends to reproduce such gendered dichotomies as masculine–feminine, public–private, reason–emotion, and violence–pacifism even as it seeks to valorize the 'feminine' side of these dualisms. Moreover, it reduces women to a unitary concept of 'woman' or 'the feminine' to promulgate *a* feminist perspective to undergird a unified politics of sisterhood. Too often, however, *the* feminist perspective elaborated by some standpoint theories is based on the experience of largely Western, white, middle-class women.[112]

A preferable alternative, they argue, is that of 'feminist postmodernism' – an orientation which avoids feminist standpoint's tendency to 'universalize' a 'particular' understanding of feminism by stressing that

the claims of every knower reflect a particular perspective shaped by social, cultural, political and personal factors and that the perspective of each knower contains blind spots, tacit presuppositions, and prejudgments of which the individual is unaware.[113]

One does not have to accept Runyan and Peterson's conclusions regarding the merits of postmodernism (and it should be clear from the critique of postmodernism offered above that the author has strong reservations in this regard) to recognize the degree to which they conform to a reflexive orientation. Not only is truth as correspondence not the deciding criterion, but reasoned arguments about the advantages and liabilities entailed by the politico-normative content of contending epistemological frameworks are central.

Nor is their intervention the only example of reflexivity in feminist theorizing. A recent response to and critique of Runyan and Peterson's endorsement of feminist postmodernism by Marysia Zalewski focuses on the liabilities of postmodernism in terms of the requirements of an emancipatory feminist critique and practice. Of particular concern, argues Zalewski, is postmodernism's 'tendency to lead towards nihilism', and its 'distaste for subject-centred enquiry and subject-based politics' which 'propels postmodernism into gender blindness'.[114] As an alternative, she suggests, following Sandra Whitworth,[115] that Critical Theory may be more in harmony – politically as well as theoretically – with the aims of an emancipatory feminism.[116]

Finally, Christine Sylvester, after reviewing the liabilities of both 'feminist standpoint' and 'feminist postmodernism', advocates an approach she terms 'postmodern feminism'.[117] This approach is marked by a method of 'empathetic cooperation', and represents a combination of the strengths of 'feminist standpoint effort to interpret the subject women, and the postmodernist effort to examine how specific subjects came to be (or not) and what they have to say'.[118] While no simple panacea, argues Sylvester, postmodern feminism and its corresponding 'socialist feminist' practice is oriented toward a

> radically empathetic conversational politics that helps us to learn the strengths and limitations of our inherited identity categories and to decide our identities, theories, politics, and daily concerns rather than to continue to derive them from, or reject them out of hand because they come from, established authority sources.[119]

Whether Sylvester's 'postmodern feminism' represents the best hope for resolving the tension 'between articulating women's voices and deconstructing gender'[120] is, of course, open to question. Whitworth has countered that while the political connections which Sylvester draws between feminist empiricism and liberal feminist politics or feminist standpoint and radical feminist politics may be clear, those she draws between postmodern feminism and social feminist politics are rather problematic. It is, notes Whitworth, 'precisely the critique rendered by socialist feminists against post-modernism that it lacks a clear and decisive politics of any sort'.[121]

Two points can be made in light of this review of feminist interventions on epistemological questions. First, the diversity of positions stands as a clear refutation of any simplistic notion that there exists a single, unambiguous 'feminist' position on the study of world politics. Just as importantly, however, the commonality of these interventions is extremely relevant in terms of the issue of reflexivity. For what is significant about Zalewski's, Sylvester's, and

Whitworth's interventions is that they, like those of Runyan and Peterson, evidence a strong concern with the identification and reasoned assessment of the politico-normative content of competing (meta-)theoretical frameworks. In sum, post-positivist feminist International Relations theorists are offering some of the most striking evidence for the growth of reflexivity in the discipline to date.

Conclusion

It may be useful to conclude by reflecting on some of the implications of a fully reflexive orientation for the members of the International Relations scholarly community on a personal, self-definitional level. As was noted, a reflexive orientation leads us to view rival paradigms as incommensurable 'coping vocabularies' linked to contending social agendas and political projects. It should also be noted that recognizing such a link greatly facilitates rationally comparing incommensurable paradigms. Simply put, once the link between 'coping vocabulary' and political project is recognized, the question of 'which paradigm is superior?' can be restated as 'which general social agenda/concrete political project is most appropriate to the global *polis*?'; the question of 'what is reliable knowledge?' can be reformulated as 'how should we live?'.

This recognition is imperative in the discipline of International Relations. Given that paradigms validate themselves in terms of both social actors and specific purposes, the question of social identity and political purpose can no longer be avoided by those who comprise the community of International Relations scholars. For if it is true that at the level of scholarship, '[paradigms] compete by virtue of the accounts they provide in explaining *what we as scholars ... define as central to our purpose, enquiry, ideology*',[122] then reflexivity directs us to a broader debate about which 'purposes', which 'enquiries' and which 'ideologies' merit the support and energy of International Relations scholars. If it is true that, to paraphrase Fichte, 'the sort of comprehensive theory one chooses depends on what sort of person one is',[123] then the question of the kind of people International Relations scholars are cannot be avoided.

To adopt a fully reflexive stance is to recognize that participating in the 'normal science' tradition of any paradigm means – consciously or not – lending support to a specific political project; it is to accept that to engage in paradigm-directed puzzle-solving is – intentionally or not – to direct one's energies to the establishment and maintenance of a specific global order. As a consequence, it becomes vital to engage in a critical examination of the relative merits of rival political projects and of contending global orders. For once it is recognized that the knowledge-defining standards that we adopt are not neutral, but have an undeniable politico-normative content, then it becomes imperative that we make a reasoned assessment of that content a central component of our deliberations about international politics.

Of course, the notion that all scholarship has a politico-normative content may well provoke significant resistance in the members of a community who have laboured hard to achieve for the discipline the title of 'science'. Such a notion runs counter to the self-image of impartial, unbiased observer of international reality. Indeed, it may even prompt the charge that reflexivity is but a veiled attempt to 'politicize the discipline'. If it does so, this would indeed be ironic. The point of reflexivity is, after all, that the study of world politics always has been informed by political agendas, and that it is time that the content of those agendas be brought out into the open and critically assessed.

To conclude, it has been argued in this chapter that the questions central to theoretical reflexivity have begun to make their appearance in contemporary theorizing about international politics, albeit at the margins of the discipline. This appearance, moveover, can be understood as signalling a potentially far-reaching restructuring of International Relations theory consistent with the emancipation-oriented tradition of critique.

Yet the restructuring of International Relations theory in a critical fashion is not restricted to the growth of theoretical reflexivity alone. It is to a second body of evidence which is indicative of a fundamental restructuring of International Relations theory – one which concerns a recognition of the central role of human consciousness in global politics – that we now turn.

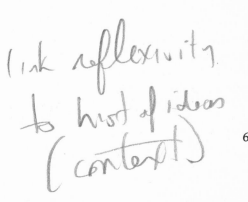

4 Human consciousness and International Relations theory

The observer ... is able, by virtue of his own rationality, to retrace the steps which politics has taken in the past and to anticipate those it will take in the future. Knowing that behind these steps there is a rational mind like his own, the observer can put himself into the place of the statesman – past, present, or future – and think as he has thought or is likely to think.
Hans J. Morgenthau[1]

But in the night of thick darkness enveloping the earliest antiquity, so remote from ourselves, there shines the eternal and never failing light of a truth beyond all question: that the world of civil society has certainly been made by men, and that its principles are therefore to be found within the modifications of our own human mind. Whoever reflects on this cannot but marvel that the philosophers ... should have neglected the study of the world of nations, or civil world, which, since men had made it, men could come to know.
Giambattista Vico[2]

Introduction

The rise of theoretical reflexivity at the margins of the discipline is not the only evidence for a restructuring of International Relations theory. In this chapter, it will be argued that a second defining characteristic of emancipatory theory derived from the Enlightenment tradition of 'critique' – an emphasis on the fundamental role of human consciousness – is also found in contemporary International Relations theory. If true, this would lend further support to the argument that there is currently a process of (meta-)theoretical 'restructuring' occurring in the discipline.

70

To that end, the present chapter will proceed as follows. In the first part of this chapter, the conventional conceptualization of human consciousness and its place within mainstream social science will be examined. It will be argued that the predominance of the positivist approach to the study of human society in mainstream social science – and in particular, the positivist tenet of the methodological unity of science – has impeded the recognition of the constitutive and transformative role of human consciousness in social and political life. It will also be argued, however, that recent developments within social and political theory – in particular, the rise of 'interpretive social science' – are challenging the positivist tenet of the methodological unity of science, thereby creating a space for the full recognition of the non-reductive power of human consciousness.

Then, in the second part of this chapter, the discipline of International Relations will be examined for parallels to social and political theory. Specifically, the conventional conceptualizations of human consciousness associated with positivist International Relations theory, as well as the rejection of those conceptualizations with the rise of 'interpretive' International Relations theory, will be reviewed. The impact that interpretive approaches, derived from the work of social and political theorists, are having on the (re-)conceptualization of the role of human consciousness within the discipline of International Relations will be presented as further evidence of the restructuring of International Relations theory in a critical, emancipatory direction.

Human consciousness in social science

In order to understand the conventional form that conceptualizations of human consciousness have taken within mainstream, positivist-dominated social science, it is important to review the major components and implications of the positivist tenet of the methodological unity of science. As was noted in chapter two, according to this tenet the research methodology developed for the study of the natural world is equally suited to the study of the social world.

It will also be remembered from our discussion of the positivist tradition in chapter two that underlying the tenet of the methodological unity of science is the assumption of 'naturalism'. That is, it is assumed that there is no fundamental difference between the social world and the natural world; the social world contains the same kind of regularities independent of time and place – in this case, 'behavioural regularities' – as exist in the natural world. It is for this reason that the approach developed to conduct a scientific analysis of the natural world – an approach designed to identify regularities and subsume them under general covering laws – is held to be equally appropriate to the social world. It is this underlying assumption of naturalism which accounts for the way human consciousness has been conceptualized and treated within mainstream social science.

At the same time, it is important to note that the positivist conceptualization of human consciousness has not gone unchallenged in contemporary social and political theory. Specifically, theorists concerned with developing and promoting an 'interpretive' approach to the study of society[3] have argued that the positivist conceptualization of human consciousness has served to obscure and misrepresent the fundamental role of human consciousness in social life.

I will begin by briefly reviewing two distinct ways that human consciousness has been conceptualized within positivist social science. I will then proceed to a review of the criticisms of positivism developed by 'interpretive' theorists. A review of the alternative formulation proposed by these theorists – and the significance of their formulation in terms of the emancipation-oriented tradition of critique – will conclude the first part of this chapter.

Positivist formulations of human consciousness

Human consciousness has been conceptualized in two distinct ways in positivist social science. The distinction between the two approaches derives from the different answers positivist social scientists have given to the question of the significance of what Weber called 'subjective meanings' – the meanings which human subjects attach to behaviour – and the value of trying to apprehend those meanings in terms of the goal of 'causal adequacy'. Depending on the answer given to this question, positivist social scientists fall into one of two camps: (i) 'strict behaviouralism' and (ii) 'meaning-oriented behaviouralism'.

'Strict behaviouralism' is the original version of the behaviouralist movement in social science, a movement representing perhaps the most concerted effort to apply the positivist tenet of the methodological unity of science to the social world. 'Strict behaviouralism' takes overt behaviour as the proper object of study. Considerable energy is directed toward achieving standardization in the measurement of human behaviour, and especially in operationalizing theoretical concepts in terms of observed behaviour. The ultimate goal, of course, is the subsumption of regularities in overt behaviour under general covering laws, themselves derived axiomatically from basic assumptions.

What then of human consciousness? What of the insistence, found in the work of Weber, for example, on the importance of the 'subjective meanings' that human beings attach to their behaviour, and of the *Verstehen* tradition in social science which orients itself toward understanding those 'subjective meanings'?

In general, strict behaviouralists hold that the understanding of 'subjective meanings' is not only not sufficient for the validation of scientific knowledge about the social world, but that 'subjective meanings' are in no way necessary to the development of scientific accounts of social life. The reasoning behind this position is simple. Scientific knowledge of the social world – positivistically conceived – must be based on empirical evidence only (i.e., publicly observable objects or events – a category into which behaviour would fall). Since the domain of human consciousness is not amenable to such observation – since the 'subjective meanings' attached to social phenomena do not exist in the public realm (but rather in the private consciousness of the individual(s) concerned) – it can have no place either as a component of reliable knowledge of the social world, or as a means of validating such knowledge (i.e., no place in the 'context of justification').

This is not to say, however, that 'strict behaviouralists' see absolutely no role for *Verstehen* in scientific investigation. Understood as a technique oriented toward 'empathetic identification' – putting oneself in the subject's shoes – *Verstehen* is regarded by strict behaviouralists as a potentially fruitful method for generating hypotheses relating external stimulus to behavioural response; a useful tool in the 'context of discovery'. In no sense, however, does the employment of interpretive techniques (i.e., *Verstehen*) affect the *logic* of social inquiry, or serve to demarcate it from the logic of the natural sciences.[4]

While all positivistically minded social scientists accept, by definition, that the 'understanding' of 'subjective meanings' has no place in the context of validation, not all would be comfortable with the notion that 'subjective meanings' themselves have no place in the scientific explanations of 'social action'. Indeed, the adherents of a second positivist formulation of human consciousness – termed here, 'meaning-oriented behaviouralism' – insist that the integration of 'subjective meanings' into social scientific accounts of human behaviour is necessary for the achievement of 'causal adequacy'.

This of course raises the question of how 'subjective meanings' are to be integrated into a scientific (i.e., positivistic) logic of investigation which stresses publicly verifiable standards of proof. Specifically, how is the social scientist to determine the exact nature of the preferences/motives/goals of the subject(s) under study?

All positivist-inspired social scientists – including those committed to integrating 'subjective meanings' into causal analysis of 'social action' – share unease with regard to variables not open to public scrutiny. As a consequence, 'meaning-oriented behaviouralists' have expended considerable effort to develop research techniques – content analysis, interviews, surveys, questionnaires – which are designed both to bring 'subjective meanings' (preferences/motives/goals) into the public realm and to facilitate standardized measurements of them. Like 'strict behaviouralists', 'meaning-oriented behaviouralists' would no doubt acknowledge that the methods of *Verstehen* ('sympathetic imagination'/'empathetic identification') have proved useful in the 'context of discovery'.[5] The final goal, however, remains the bringing of 'subjective meanings' attached to social action into the public realm, so that they can be treated as 'intervening variables' between the 'stimulus' (the action context) and the 'response' (behaviour).

By correlating particular beliefs/motivations/values with a particular behaviour in a particular context, it becomes possible to 'derive empirically testable hypotheses about uniformities of behaviour under specific conditions'.[6] In this way, argue 'meaning-oriented behaviouralists', the importance of 'subjective meanings' in 'social action' can be accommodated without violating the positivist standard of 'causal adequacy'.[7]

The suitability of 'meaning-oriented behaviouralism' in terms of the goal of positivist social science is clear. By integrating 'subjective meaning' into regularities linking context and behaviour, and by devising ways of ensuring that those variables remain open to public scrutiny by the members of the scientific community, this approach conforms completely to the positivist tenet of the methodological unity of science. In short, while the 'subjective meanings' attached to behaviour would seem to require a modicum of innovation at the level of research techniques, 'meaning-oriented behaviouralists' – like 'strict behaviouralists' – do not see the 'meaningfulness' of social life as necessitating any qualitative change at the level of the positivistic logic of investigation.

It is this view – and the assumption of naturalism of which it is the expression – that is the prime focus of criticism of those wishing to promote an alternative to positivist approaches to the study of social life. It is to their criticisms – and their alternative formulation – that we now turn.

Beyond positivism: human consciousness as constitutive of social life

We have seen in our brief review of conventional positivist-inspired treatments of human consciousness in the social sciences that consciousness has been conceptualized as 'subjective meaning' which either has relevance only in heuristic terms in the 'context of discovery' or which is integrated into scientific investigation as an 'intervening variable' between context and behaviour. In either case, the dimension of human consciousness in social life does not pose any challenge to the assumption of naturalism which underlies the positivist tenet of the methodological unity of science. That is, human consciousness is not seen to raise any challenge to the idea that regularities independent of time and place exist in the social world in the same way as they do in the natural world.

It is the positivist accommodation of human consciousness to the assumption of naturalism that theorists advocating an interpretive approach to the study of society reject. It is important to be clear about the exact nature of the challenge posed by the interpretive approach to positivist social science. Interpretive theorists do not deny that behavioural regularities exist in the social world. Nor do they contest that individuals attach 'subjective meanings' to their behaviour.

What interpretive theorists contest is that the behavioural regularities which can be observed in the social world exist independently of time and place as they do in the natural world. What they also contest is that the notion of 'subjective meanings' attached by individuals to their behaviour is an adequate conceptualization of human consciousness in social life.

Interpretive theorists start with the understanding that human beings are 'fundamentally self-interpreting and self-defining'.[8] That is, human beings live in a world of cultural meaning which has its source in their own interpretations of that world; human beings act in the context of a 'web of meaning' – a web that they themselves have spun. As a consequence, the social world – in contrast to the natural world – 'is itself partly constituted by self-interpretation'.[9]

The fundamental dimension of self-interpretation in the social world has important consequences for social science. As a consequence, argue interpretive theorists, the objects of study of social science must include the interpretations and definitions of the human subjects whose interaction makes up the social world. Social science, then, is interpretive in a double sense. On one level, it is, like any knowledge-generating activity, an interpretive enterprise.[10] What distinguishes it from interpretations of the natural world, however, is that an important part of the subject matter of social science is itself an interpretation – the self-interpretation of the human beings under study.[11]

The 'web of meaning' spun by human beings is fundamental to the nature of their behaviour. For it is the 'web of meaning' which makes the behavioural regularities observed in the social world what they are – that is, *human* practices – and distinguishes them from the non-human regularities observed in the natural world.[12] And it is for this reason, affirm interpretive theorists, that the practices in which human beings are engaged cannot be studied in isolation from the 'web of meaning', which is, in a fundamental sense, constitutive of those practices, even as it is embedded in and instantiated through those same practices.

It is clear then, that while interpretive theorists may agree that behavioural regularities are an identifiable feature of the social world, they would nonetheless oppose 'strict behaviouralism's' exclusive focus on actions 'that are supposedly brute-data-identifiable'[13] to the neglect of the 'web of meaning' constitutive of and embedded in those actions. But what of the alternative offered by 'meaning-oriented behaviouralists'? Does not their approach, which renders the concern with 'meaning' compatible with the positivist goal of subsuming behavioural regularities under general covering laws, meet the concerns of interpretive theorists?

Interpretive theorists deny that it does. The approach of 'meaning-oriented behaviouralists' is not satisfactory, argue interpretive theorists, because of the way it conceptualizes both the 'web of meaning' and the relationship of the 'web of meaning' to human practices.

Specifically, 'meaning-oriented behaviouralism' conceives of the 'web of meaning' as the sum-total of the 'subjective meanings' of the individuals involved. And it conceives of the relationship between the 'web of meaning' and human practices as a correspondence of specific 'subjective meanings' to specific actions – a correspondence which allows for the establishment of verifiable correlations compatible with causal explanation.

Once again, it must be stressed that an interpretive approach has no more difficulty accepting that individuals may attach 'subjective meaning' to their actions than it does acknowledging that behavioural regularities may be identified in the social world. What an interpretive approach contests, however, is: (i) that the 'web of meaning' should be understood as the sum-total of individual 'subjective meanings', and (ii) that the relationship between the 'web of meaning' and human practice is one of correspondence.

Interpretive theorists, in contrast to 'meaning-oriented behaviouralists', conceive of the 'web of meaning' not as a sum-total of 'subjective meanings' which grow out of individual self-interpretations and self-definitions, but rather as being comprised of 'intersubjective meanings' which are the product of the collective self-interpretations and self-definitions of human communities. These 'intersubjective meanings', moreover, are not the same as the positivist notion of a 'consensus' about beliefs or values. As Charles Taylor notes,

> When we speak of consensus we speak of beliefs and values which could be the property of a single person, or many, or all; but intersubjective meanings could not be the property of a single person because they are rooted in social practice.[14]

Furthermore, the relationship between the 'intersubjective meanings' which make up the 'web of meaning' and human practices is not one of correlation, where 'intersubjective meanings' serve as an 'intervening variable' in a causal sequence. Rather, the 'intersubjective meanings' are constitutive of those practices.

There is no question that positivist-dominated social science has great difficulty in coping with this notion of 'intersubjective meanings'. As Taylor has noted in a discussion of positivist political science,

> Intersubjective meanings, ways of experiencing in society which are expressed in the language and descriptions constitutive of institutions and practices, do not fit into the categorical grid of mainstream

Consensus as a positivist notion

77

political science. This allows only for an intersubjective reality that is brute-data-identifiable. But social practices and institutions that are partly constituted by certain ways of talking about them are not so identifiable. We have to understand the language, the underlying meanings that constitute them.[15]

This is not to deny that 'subjective meanings' can be placed in a relationship of covariance with specific actions. Notes Taylor,

We can allow, once we accept a certain set of institutions or practices as our starting point and not as objects of further questioning, that we can easily take as brute data that certain acts are judged to take place or certain states judged to hold within a semantic field of these practices – for instance, that someone has voted Liberal or signed the petition. We can then go on to correlate certain subjective meanings – beliefs, attitudes, and so forth – with this behaviour or its lack.[16]

But this approach has serious – and from the perspective of interpretive theorists, pernicious – consequences for social science. Continues Taylor,

But this means that we give up trying to define further just what these practices and institutions are, what the meanings are which they require and hence sustain. For these meanings do not fit into the grid; they are not subjective beliefs or values, but are constitutive of social reality. In order to get at them we have to drop the basic premise that social reality is made up of brute data alone ... We have to admit that intersubjective social reality has to be partly defined in terms of meanings; that meanings as subjective are not just in causal interaction with a social reality made up of brute data, but that as intersubjective they are constitutive of this reality.[17]

An example provided by Taylor may serve to illustrate the points being made here. Let us take the case of negotiation, a form of social interaction familiar to the inhabitants of liberal, capitalist societies. First, it is quite plausible that behavioural regularities might exist in negotiation settings, and that furthermore, 'strict behaviouralists' might succeed in identifying those regularities. It is also true, virtually by definition, that different parties in a negotiation setting will have different subjective motivations, goals, and values, and that 'meaning-oriented behaviouralists' might succeed both in identifying those 'subjective meanings' and in establishing significant correlations between them and specific actions (e.g., negotiating positions).

What interpretive theorists stress, however, is that those behavioural regularities and those diverging 'subjective meanings' are dependent upon the existence of negotiation as a social practice for their very possibility. Moreover, negotiation, as a social practice, is itself constituted by a specific set of 'intersubjective meanings'.

> The actors may have all sorts of beliefs and attitudes which may be rightly thought of as their individual beliefs and attitudes, even if others share them; they may subscribe to certain policy goals or certain forms of theory about the polity, or feel resentment at certain things, and so on. They bring these with them into their negotiations, and strive to satisfy them. But what they do not bring into the negotiation is the set of ideas and norms constitutive of negotiations themselves. These must be the common property of the society before there can be any question of anyone entering into negotiation or not. Hence they are not subjective meanings, the property of one or some individuals, but rather intersubjective meanings, which are constitutive of the social matrix in which individuals find themselves and act.[18]

The 'intersubjective meanings' which constitute the practice of negotiation are very specific. Notes Taylor:

> Our whole notion of negotiation is bound up ... with the distinct identity and autonomy of the parties, with the willed nature of their relations; it is a very contractual notion.[19]

These particular 'intersubjective meanings', moreover, are themselves context specific. As Taylor notes, the set of 'intersubjective meanings' which constitute the practice of negotiation and bargaining, are not present in every society:

> But other societies have no such conception. It is reported about the traditional Japanese village that the foundation of its social life was a powerful form of consensus, which put a high premium on unanimous decision. Such a consensus would be considered shattered if two clearly articulated parties were to separate out, pursuing opposed aims and attempting either to vote down the opposition or to push it into a settlement on the most favourable possible terms for themselves. Discussion there must be, and some kind of adjustment of differences. But our idea of bargaining, with the assumption of distinct autonomous parties in willed relationship, has no place there.[20]

As a consequence, the naturalist assumption that regularities in the social world – conceived independently of or in causal relation to individual 'subjective meanings' – are, like regularities in the natural world, independent of time and place, must be rejected. By extension, the positivist tenet of the methodological unity of science can no longer be sustained.

It is important to be clear about the argument that is being advanced by the interpretive theorists. Two points, in particular, merit stressing. First, while it is true that an interpretive approach stands opposed to positivism's 'mechanical materialism', it would be a mistake to conclude that what it proposes as an alternative is a return to a radical form of idealism (i.e., that the world is a creation of mind). It would be a mistake, first, because interpretive theorists have consistently argued that just as human practices are always constituted by a 'web of meaning', so also a 'web of meaning' is always embedded in, and instantiated through, concrete human practices. Thus, just as practices cannot be understood apart from the 'web of meaning' which constitutes them, neither can a 'web of meaning' be understood in isolation from the practices in which it is embedded. Furthermore, an interpretive approach does not imply idealism because such an approach recognizes that the process of self-reflection and self-interpretation always takes place in relation to a concrete historical context (material and social).

The second point which needs to be stressed – and at somewhat greater length than the first – is that an interpretive approach should not be equated with what might be termed the 'hermeneutics of recovery'. That is, it should not be understood as advocating that: (i) the true subject matter of social science is individual consciousness; (ii) the appropriate methodology for the researcher is one of empathy; and (iii) the appropriate goal of social science is one of 'recovering' the original 'intentions' of human agents. The interpretive approach 'emphatically refutes the claim that one can somehow reduce the complex world of signification to the products of self-consciousness in the traditional philosophical sense'.[21] As noted above, interpretive theorists do not argue that the object of investigation is individual consciousness (subjective meaning), but rather the 'web of meaning' – 'the web of language, symbol, and institutions that constitutes signification'[22] – comprised of 'intersubjective meanings'. As a consequence, 'intentionality' – like human behaviour itself – is understood to be 'dependent on the prior existence of the shared world of meaning within which the subjects of human discourse constitute themselves'.[23]

As a consequence, 'empathy' is not seen as an appropriate methodology for an interpretive approach. For empathy is a methodology oriented to gaining access to private consciousness. But as noted above, the 'intersubjective meanings' are not confined to the realm of private consciousness. They are embedded in and instantiated through social practices which are part of the public realm. Note Rabinow and Sullivan:

> Meanings or norms 'are not just in the minds of the actors but are out there in the practices themselves; practices which cannot be conceived as a set of individual actions, but which are essentially modes of social relations, or mutual action.' These meanings are intersubjective; they are not reducible to individual subjective psychological states, beliefs, or propositions. They are neither subjective nor objective but what lies behind both.[24]

Instead of empathy, the methodology appropriate to an interpretive approach can be described as the 'hermeneutic circle'. By 'hermeneutic circle' is meant that the social scientist endeavours to 'make sense' of the social world by demonstrating that 'there is a coherence between the actions of the agent and the meaning of his situation for him'.[25] 'Making sense' of the social world, then, involves a process of 'testing' the adequacy of a proffered 'reading', that is (i) of the 'web of meaning' in terms of the concrete social practices in which it is embedded, and (ii) of the 'coherence' of observed social practices in terms of the 'web of meaning' which constitutes those practices.[26] As a consequence, the interpretation of a given 'web of meaning'/social practice can never be tested against an objective standard. Rather, the testing and refinement of particular interpretations is always done in terms of other interpretations. It is never possible to escape the 'hermeneutic circle'.[27]

And finally, to conclude this second point, it would not be correct to equate an interpretive approach with a 'hermeneutics of recovery' because the objective of social science for those committed to an interpretive approach is not limited to 'recovering' the self-interpretations and self-definitions which constitute social practices.[28] Because social practices are constituted by 'intersubjective meanings', 'recovering' those meanings – by means of the 'hermeneutic circle' – is an important step.[29] Yet as is apparent from Taylor's statements that 'social reality has to be *partly* defined in terms of meanings',[30] that 'that of which we are trying to find the coherence is itself *partly* constituted by self-interpretation',[31] an interpretive approach is quite capable of accepting that the subject matter of social science extends beyond 'webs of meaning'.

Rather, the objective of an interpretive approach is to re-express the relationship between 'intersubjective meanings', which derive from self-interpretation and self-definition, and the social practices in which they are embedded and which they constitute – in short, the 'form of life' – in order to exercise critical judgment.[32] In short, the goal of an interpretive social science is not to restate the understanding of the human agents involved, but to 'attain[] greater clarity than the immediate understanding of agent or observer'.[33]

We have seen that the notion of 'intersubjective meanings' associated with an interpretive approach to the study of the social world offers an alternative to the positivist conceptualization of 'meaning' in social life as either an 'heuristic aid' or as 'subjective meanings' which can be correlated to specific actions. We have also seen how the alternative offered by an interpretive approach challenges the positivist tenet of the methodological unity of science by undermining the assumption of naturalism. In this way, interpretive social science opens a space for conceiving of human consciousness as both constitutive and potentially transformative of the social world – a development very much in keeping with the emancipation-oriented tradition of critical theory.

The question remains, however, to what extent, if any, the insights of interpretive social theory are being applied in the discipline of International Relations. Specifically, to what extent, if any, is an alternative to positivist conceptualizations of human consciousness in International Relations theory being offered? To what extent is a parallel space for conceiving of human consciousness as both constitutive and potentially transformative of international politics being created? It is to these questions that we now turn.

International Relations theory and the question of human consciousness

Positivist formulations of human consciousness in International Relations theory

On the basis of our review of positivist formulations in the first part of this chapter, it is now possible to place positivist formulations of human consciousness in International Relations theory in a larger meta-theoretical context. We shall begin with a review of the methodological pronouncements of an individual who, it can be argued, serves as a model for positivist theorists working within the discipline of International Relations. Specifically, we will begin with a look at the work of Hans Morgenthau.

On consecutive pages of the classic *Politics Among Nations*, Morgenthau makes the following two statements:

> Political realism believes that politics, like society in general, is governed by objective laws that have their roots in human nature ... The operation of these laws being impervious to our preferences, men will challenge them only at the risk of failure.[34]

> For realism, theory consists in ascertaining facts and giving them meaning through reason ... To give meaning to the factual raw material of foreign policy, we must approach political reality with a kind of rational outline, a map that suggests to us the possible meanings of foreign policy. In other words, we put ourselves in the position of a statesman who must meet a certain problem of foreign policy under certain circumstances ... We assume that statesmen think and act in terms of interest defined as power ... That assumption allows us to retrace and anticipate ... the steps a statesman – past, present, or future – has taken or will take on the political scene. We look over his shoulder when he writes his dispatches; we listen in on his conversation with other statesmen; we read and anticipate his very thoughts.[35]

This raises the question of how one is to understand the relationship between these two statements. One possible response is to follow Ashley in arguing that Morgenthau's work – and the realist tradition in general – is marked by 'genuine antinomies', and 'critical tensions'.[36] The root of these 'antinomies/tensions', according to Ashley, lies in the fact that Morgenthau's work attempts to unite two distinct and mutually opposed methodological traditions: specifically, positivism (as expressed in Morgenthau's first statement) and interpretive theory – *Verstehen* (as expressed in the second). The interpretive tradition is in evidence in Morgenthau's admonition to put ourselves in the place of the statesman – to adopt 'the historian's pose peering over the statesman's shoulder, listening in on his conversations, and anticipating his thoughts'.[37] The positivist approach, on the other hand, is visible in Morgenthau's affirmations that '[international] politics is governed by objective laws' which are 'impervious to our preferences'.

If Ashley is correct, it would seem to pose a major problem in terms of the coherence of Morgenthau's contribution to the foundations of the discipline. As George has argued, however, there is good reason to question this interpretation.[38] It is important to recognize that Ashley's identification of antinomies/tensions within Morgenthau is dependent on equating an interpretive approach with the techniques of empathetic identification associated with *Verstehen*. Yet as was noted in the first part of this chapter, *Verstehen*'s emphasis on private, subjective meanings stands in stark contrast to interpretive social science's concern with public, intersubjective meanings. On the other hand, positivists have had little difficulty in incorporating *Verstehen* into positivist research. Specifically, positivists have remained faithful to the tenet of the methodological unity of science and the assumption of naturalism by employing *Verstehen* as a technique potentially relevant to the context of discovery, and by subordinating its results to the methods appropriate to the testing of hypotheses in the context of justification.

In short, it can be argued that the two statements by Morgenthau noted above are less a sign of antinomies/tensions in his work than evidence that from Morgenthau onward mainstream International Relations theorists have accommodated *Verstehen* techniques to their positivist-inspired study of world politics in the same way as mainstream theorists in social science more generally[39] – they have redefined *Verstehen* as a technique potentially relevant to the context of discovery and subordinated it to the methods appropriate to the testing of hypotheses in the context of justification.[40]

This is not to say that all positivist-minded International Relations scholars have taken the same stance regarding human consciousness. For as in the case of positivist social science more generally, it can be argued that to mainstream International Relations theory's reconciliation of 'subjective meanings' to the exigencies of the positivist tradition correspond two distinct positivist formulations in International Relations.

On the one hand one finds those International Relations theorists who correspond to our discussion of 'strict behaviouralism' in the first part of this chapter. These scholars followed Morgenthau in affirming that the central focus of the study of international politics must be 'the examination of political acts performed'.[41] Dominated as the discipline has been by realist assumptions,[42] it comes as no surprise that the political acts focused upon were performed by states.

The realist-inspired 'strict behaviouralists' congregated to form one of the two main approaches to the study of international politics: that of 'systems theory'. From this perspective, states were treated as billiard balls, operating in a system.[43] Moreover, in keeping with the general orientation of 'strict behaviouralism', it was assumed that 'the perceptions of the actors ... [were] essentially irrelevant to the task of explanation'.[44]

Others, however, appealed to Morgenthau's (and Weber's) assertions to argue that while the examination of the behavioural facts of international politics – the 'political acts performed' – was vital, the 'examination of the facts is not enough'. They followed Morgenthau in affirming that

> To give meaning to the factual raw material of foreign policy, we must approach political reality with a kind of rational outline, a map that suggests to us the *possible meanings* of foreign policy. In other words, we put ourselves in the position of a statesman.[45]

That is, these theorists – corresponding to the category of 'meaning-oriented behaviouralists' – affirm that the 'subjective meanings' attached to 'political acts performed' were a vital component of the development of scientific *explanations* of those acts. In the words of Philip Lawrence, 'In judging and explaining foreign policy decision-making, the most crucial elements that must be evaluated are purposes and motives.'[46] And once again, reflecting the realist hegemony in the discipline, the behaviour in question is that of the leaders of states, while the 'subjective meanings' – the 'purposes and motives' – to be evaluated are those attached by these state managers to their actions.

If the 'strict behaviouralists' in the discipline of International Relations were to be found in the 'systems theorists' camp, 'meaning-oriented behaviouralists', as suggested by the Lawrence quote above, tended to gravitate to that of 'foreign policy analysis'.[47] Here the attempt to determine the 'subjective meanings' attached by state managers to their actions took a variety of forms employing a wide range of creative methodological techniques. These ranged from 'the image',[48] to 'belief systems',[49] to 'operational codes',[50] to 'cognitive maps',[51] to 'lessons of the past',[52] to 'Brecher's research design'[53] in the case of form, and included techniques such as 'content analysis' and questionnaires.[54] The underlying commonality which unites these approaches, however, is adoption of the 'subjectivist' position[55] – that is, the concern with identifying the 'subjective meanings' attached to international behaviour and with bringing those meanings into the public realm. As with 'meaning-oriented behaviouralism' in general, the 'subjective meanings' of state managers – their 'perceptions' and 'beliefs' – were understood as intervening variables – a 'filtering device'[56] – between the empirical reality of the international context and international behaviour. And in keeping with the positivist tenet of the methodological unity of science, it was the position of 'meaning-oriented behaviouralists' in the discipline of International Relations that if the 'perceptions [of state managers] could be studied and if significant regularities could be found, then here was another route to [scientific] International Relations theory'.[57]

As with treatments of human consciousness in positivist social science in general, then, in positivist International Relations theory the realm of human consciousness is conceptualized as either an 'heuristic aid' in the context of discovery, or as a significant 'intervening variable' which can be correlated to specific behaviour in specific contexts. What this shows is that positivist International Relations theorists were just as determined to assimilate human consciousness to the tenet of the methodological unity of science in accordance with the assumption of naturalism which underlies it. As a consequence, positivist International Relations theory – whether 'strict behaviouralist' or 'meaning-oriented behaviouralist' – is fundamentally unable to appreciate the constitutive and potentially transformative nature of human consciousness in terms of the global order.

There is, however, an alternative formulation of human consciousness in International Relations theory – a formulation which draws not upon positivism, but upon interpretive social science for its inspiration – which does not suffer from positivism's limitations. It is to that alternative formulation that we now turn.

Interpretive approaches to the study of international world politics

The issue of 'interpretive' approaches to the study of International Relations has achieved prominence in recent meta-theoretical discussions of the discipline. In his 1988 International Studies Association presidential address, Robert Keohane noted that the work of interpretive theorists, such as Hayward Alker, Richard Ashley, Friedrich

Kratochwil, John Ruggie, and Robert Cox, now provides a clear alternative to the mainstream, positivist-inspired approach to the study of International Relations in general, and international institutions in particular.[58]

Given the preceding discussion of the differences between positivist and interpretive social science, and given the traditional predominance of positivist research in International Relations, we are now well placed to understand both the distinctiveness and unorthodox nature of interpretive approaches to the study of International Relations. We can, for example, grasp the significance of Keohane's observation that an interpretive approach to the study of international institutions is marked by an emphasis on the 'importance of the '*intersubjective meanings*' of international institutional activity',[59] and that such an approach 'stresses the impact of human subjectivity and the embeddedness of contemporary international institutions in pre-existing practices'.[60]

Given that attention to the constitutive role of human consciousness is a defining characteristic of critical theory, the rise of interpretive approaches would seem a clear indication that International Relations theory is undergoing a process of restructuring. Here it will be argued that though such a conclusion is warranted, it must also be recognized that not all applications of interpretive social science in the discipline serve emancipatory aims. To make this point, let us turn our attention to the sub-field of International Organization.

In the 1980s, neorealist-inspired analysis of international organization dominated much of the field of International Relations. The substantive concern of this approach was the institutionalized co-operative behaviour existing among advanced capitalist states in the context of the Liberal International Economic Order (LIEO). The approach featured a focus on the monetary and trade institutions – the 'regimes' – which regulated that order, where regimes were defined as

> implicit or explicit principles, norms, rules, and decision-making procedures around which actors' expectations converge in a given area of International Relations.[61]

This definition was well-suited to neorealism's self-consciously positivist orientation. The traditional concern with 'prevailing practices', 'behaviour', and 'action', lent itself well to analysis according to the approach of 'strict behaviouralism', while the emphasis on 'expectations' and 'beliefs' seemed to leave open the possibility of a 'meaning-oriented behaviouralist' analysis of regimes.[62]

In time, however, some scholars began to sense the inherent limitations of the positivist approach to the study of international institutions. The prime difficulty lay in a disjuncture between 'ontology and epistemology' – that is, between the nature of international institutions and the dominant modes of analysis. Specifically, it was argued by interpretive theorists such as Kratochwil and Ruggie that difficulties in understanding the workings of regimes – when they were present and when not, and how they changed over time – arose because of the incompatibility between on the one hand an intersubjectively constituted object of study requiring an interpretive method and study and, on the other, a positivist method of study premised on the assumption of naturalism.[63]

Given this analysis of the difficulties in positivist regime analysis, the solution was clear: the resolution of the problems in the analysis of regimes, affirmed Kratochwil and Ruggie, 'will require the incorporation into prevailing approaches of insights and methods derived from the interpretive sciences'.[64] In short, interpretive social science was seen to offer an important contribution to the resolution of a number of fundamental anomalies in the neorealist analysis of regimes.[65]

Despite their important insights, however, it can be argued that Kratochwil and Ruggie's discussion of the potential contribution of an interpretive approach is incomplete. For the contribution of the approach is, in their view, limited in its scope. Interpretive epistemologies will not be required, they conclude,

> in circumstances that require little interpretation on the part of the relevant actors – because the environment is placid, because shared knowledge prevails, or because coercion determines outcomes.[66]

It is important to stress that in limiting interpretive approaches in this way, Kratochwil and Ruggie are departing from one of the main insights of interpretive social science, namely that all social practices – whether they occur in an environment that is 'placid' or overtly coercive in nature – are constituted through intersubjective meanings; that all social activity requires interpretation both by immediate participants and by those seeking to analyse that activity in a systematic fashion.[67]

Indeed, it can be argued that a second contribution of interpretive social science to realist theorizing is exactly this: to re-establish the fundamental commonality between institutions regulating interaction in the realm of 'low politics',[68] and institutions regulating interaction in the realm of 'high politics'. And in this regard, it is noteworthy that one of the most recent and most extensive discussions of interpretive social science and the study of international politics – Hollis and Smith's *Explaining and Understanding International Relations*[69] – extends the purview of interpretive approaches to include the realm of 'high politics'.

Hollis and Smith draw on Winch's Wittgensteinian formulation of interpretive social science as the exploration of intersubjectively recognized rules constituting 'games',[70] affirming that the approach has much to offer in the study of international politics. It can be argued, of course, that the 'power of tanks and missiles is not the internal authority of an abbot', and that 'moving a nuclear submarine is different from moving a castle in chess'.[71] Even so, argue Hollis and Smith, there are interesting similarities between the arena of international politics – including the realm of 'high politics' – and games in a Wittgensteinian sense:

> Nuclear submarines function as threats and bargaining counters: the abbot's authority may have something to do with threats of hell-fire. Unless some kind of international society had been constructed, there could be no United Nations, with its Assembly and its fragile but often effective agencies.[72]

Thus, affirm Hollis and Smith,

> The more the constructed arena of international diplomacy matters for what nations are enabled and constrained to do, the more it is worth thinking of the arena as a place where Wittgensteinian games are played.[73]

In short, interpretive social science directs us to see that the coercive state practices which make up the 'balance of power' can and should be analysed in the same way as one would analyse the liberal trade and monetary practices associated with the LIEO – by analysing them to uncover the intersubjective meanings which constitute those practices and which are simultaneously instantiated through them.[74]

It would seem, then, that interpretive social science contains important resources for reforming and revitalizing realist theorizing about international politics. And so it does, but only at the cost of artificially restricting the scope of the practice of interpretation. In fact, and *pace* the efforts of Kratochwil, Ruggie, Hollis, and Smith, while interpretive approaches can be used to refurbish realist theorizing, they are even more ideally suited to challenge it.

To understand the potential an interpretive approach holds for challenging the realist mainstream, it is necessary to consider standard objections to progress in the realm of international politics. Specifically, the long-held realist opposition to the development of 'progressivist' approaches to international politics derives not only from the emphasis upon the conflictual nature of international politics (war of all against all), but also from the essentially positivistic characterization of the international order as fundamentally unchanging (and hence fundamentally unchangeable).[75] It is a direct consequence of the unchanging nature of the global order, argue realists, that International Relations theory can never be a theory of the 'good life', but only a theory of 'survival'.

Of course, the realist formulation did traditionally allow for the possibility that human practice might mitigate some of the worst effects of the global order. Many realists accept that international institutions can play an important role in regulating the global orders in which they are 'nested'[76] – the capitalist world economy in the case of trade and monetary regimes; the anarchical Westphalian system of states in the case of the balance of power.

As was noted above, interpretive approaches can be used to achieve new insights into the constitution and functioning of regulatory international institutions. It must also be recognized, however, that interpretive approaches offer more than just a means for understanding the constitution and functioning of regulatory international institutions. They can be used as well to generate insights into the very orders in which regulatory international institutions are embedded.

The uniqueness of interpretive social science is the insight it provides into the fact that the *totality* of social existence is an ongoing process of self-interpretation and self-definition by human collectivities. Consequently, not only the regulatory institutions but the underlying world orders themselves are comprised of social practices, are themselves constituted by and instantiating intersubjective meanings.

It is in this regard that interpretive approaches provide a welcome antidote to realism's positivist-reinforced pessimism about the possibility for progress. To reiterate, interpretive social science maintains, in opposition to naturalistic orientations, that all social and political orders – including the global order – are the products of social practices. In short, from the perspective of interpretive social science, both the LIEO and international anarchy can be seen as constituted by intersubjective meanings.[77]

It has been the concern of a small but growing number of interpretively oriented International Relations scholars, moreover, to identify these meanings. Among the intersubjective meanings which constitute the contemporary global order are the notions that

> people are organized and commanded by states which have authority over defined territories; that states relate to one another through diplomatic agents; that certain rules apply for the protection of diplomatic agents as being in the common interest of all states; and that certain kinds of behaviour are to be expected when conflict arises between states, such as negotiation, confrontation, or war.[78]

In this regard, the contribution of postmodern International Relations scholars has been considerable. Postmodernists in the discipline have been particularly effective in exploring and 'deconstructing' intersubjective meanings fundamental to the modern global order such as sovereignty, anarchy, and foreign policy.[79]

Also included in the intersubjective meanings that constitute the global order are the 'packages of expectations' which define masculine and feminine identities (i.e., gender). And here it is important to take note of the contribution of feminist theorists in excavating and rendering these meanings explicit. Their particular focus has been on meanings relating to gender, and the way in which those meanings both inform and are instantiated through institutions and practices as varied as the national security state, networks of military bases, diplomacy, tourist, and international organizations.[80]

Given this understanding of the nature of the global order, it is clear how interpretive approaches offer support for notions of progressive and emancipatory change. The intersubjective meanings which constitute the global order are themselves the product of an on-going process of self-definition and self-reflection; they are, then, like the practices which instantiate them, open to change.[81]

Finally, in anticipation of a common objection to interpretive approaches raised by positivists, it is important to recognize that an interpretive perspective does not deny that regularized behaviour patterns have characterized much of international politics (e.g., power-seeking states, power-balancing interactions). The point is not to deny the existence of the behavioural regularities that positivistic analysis has identified in the social world, but rather

> to determine when theoretical statements grasp invariant regularities of social action as such and when they express ideologically frozen relations of dependence that can in principle be transformed.[82]

The notion of regularized behaviour in the global order as an expression not of natural necessity, but of 'ideologically frozen relations of dependence', also has consequences for our understanding of mainstream theorizing in International Relations. It moves us to effect a reappraisal of Keohane's observation that

> Realist and neorealist theories are avowedly rationalistic, accepting ... a 'substantive' conception of rationality, characterizing 'behaviour that can be adjudged objectively to be optimally adapted to the situation'.[83]

For once one sees the 'situation' not as a 'given' reality but rather as a socially constructed order, then it is possible to see the regulative ideal of 'substantive rationality' in a rather different light – not as a neutral formulation capturing a timeless, universalized thought-process, but rather as a self-limiting form of 'instrumental rationality' severely circumscribed in its capacity for fundamental self-reflection. Similarly, it lends additional support to understanding traditional positivist-informed International Relations theory not as a neutral body of knowledge, but as a form of 'traditional theory' having the function of facilitating the 'adaptation' of human beings to their basic circumstances, no matter how violence-prone or inequitable.[84] In short, positivist-inspired mainstream International Relations theory can be seen as a major social force contributing to the maintenance of 'ideologically frozen relations of dependence', an effect it accomplishes through the 'reification' of the global order, in other words by presenting that order as a 'thing' standing apart from and independent of human will or action.

Indeed, not only does the notion of 'substantive rationality' appear in a new light, but so do the efforts to supplement the traditional, realist/positivist-inspired approach to the study of International Relations noted above. For while it is true that the efforts of mainstream interpretive theorists such as Ruggie, Kratochwil, Hollis, and Smith help to dereify the international institutions which regulate the global order(s), their failure to recognize that an interpretive analysis can be extended beyond a study of regulatory international institutions to include the global orders in which those institutions are 'nested' has an important consequence. Ultimately, that failure serves to reinforce the notion that the global order is natural and fixed; a reality to be accommodated and even accepted. Consequently, not only can traditional, positivist-inspired theorizing be seen as a form of 'traditional theory', but so can much of interpretively oriented theorizing about international politics as well.[85]

It is this perspective on traditional, positivist-inspired theorizing – as well as on recent efforts to supplement that theorizing with an interpretively derived analysis of regulative international institutions – that gives the effort to develop an emancipation-oriented interpretive theory of International Relations its distinctive character. For it is a central tenet of such theorizing that an interpretive analysis of regulative international institutions cannot be conducted independently of an interpretive analysis of the global order itself, and that the latter cannot be effectuated successfully without attention being paid to the 'ideological' component of the reproduction of that order.[86] In short, from this perspective, change in the global order is dependent upon mounting a challenge to the 'ideologically frozen relations of dependence' which sustain it.[87] This raises the question of the kind of practice which is suited to such a challenge. It is that question we will take up in the chapter which follows.

Conclusion

This chapter began by exploring the issue of human consciousness in terms of social and political theory. It was argued that the predominance of the positivist approach to the study of human society in mainstream social science – in particular, the positivist tenet of the methodological unity of science – has impeded the recognition of the constitutive and potentially transformative role of human consciousness in social and political life. It was also argued, however, that the rise of interpretive approaches to the study of society have challenged positivism's hegemony, and have created a space for the full recognition of the non-reductive power of human consciousness.

Then, in the second part of this chapter, the discipline of International Relations was examined in the light of the developments in social and political theory. It was argued that once again, despite the predominance of positivist formulations of human consciousness in International Relations theory, the rise of interpretive approaches in the discipline is undeniable. Furthermore, despite the objections that have been raised – and continue to be raised[88] – there is good reason to believe that interpretive approaches will not be easily dislodged from contemporary International Relations theory. Finally, and most importantly, interpretive approaches to the study of International Relations are serving not only to reform and reinvigorate established traditions such as realism, they are also being employed to underscore the possibility of a radical, emancipatory transformation of the global order.

As a consequence, it can be argued that the same space for the recognition of the constitutive and transformative role of human consciousness that has been created in contemporary social science – a recognition which stands as one of the three defining characteristics of critical theory – is being created in the discipline of International Relations. If true, this is further evidence for the 'restructuring' of International Relations theory in a more critical, emancipation-oriented direction.

5　International Relations theory and social criticism

> Hence, a theory of politics presents not only a guide to under-
> standing, but also an ideal for action. It presents a map of the
> political scene not only in order to understand what that scene is
> like, but also in order to show the shortest and safest road to a given
> objective. The use of theory, then, is not limited to rational
> explanation and anticipation. A theory of politics also contains a
> normative element. Hans J. Morgenthau[1]

> True, the rationality of pure science is value-free and does not
> stipulate any practical ends, it is 'neutral' to any extraneous values
> that may be imposed upon it. But this neutrality is a *positive*
> character. Herbert Marcuse[2]

Introduction

In the preceding two chapters, we have reviewed the evidence for a
critical restructuring of International Relations theory in terms of
reflexivity and the conceptualization of human consciousness. There
remains, however, one defining characteristic of critical theory that
has not yet been discussed in relation to contemporary theorizing
about International Relations. This is critical theory's engagement in
social criticism in support of practical political activity for the
transformation of established 'forms of life'.

It is the task of the present chapter to address this issue. As some of
the issues central to this task have already been encountered, this
chapter will proceed somewhat differently from the previous two.
After noting the centrality of the tenet of value-freedom in the

discipline of International Relations, I will review arguments in support of the tenet. I will then attempt to counter these arguments by identifying the 'hidden normative content' of the positivist quest. I shall do so, first, by recalling points made in the previous two chapters, and then by focusing on a third aspect not yet developed: the relation of theory to practice.

The implications of positivism's 'hidden normative content' will be taken up in terms of two issues with wide implications for the discipline. First, there is the issue of renewed interest in 'normative International Relations theory'. As in previous chapters, my concern will not be primarily theoretical. That is, I will not be concerned so much with the very worthy issue of contending normative theories and their application to concrete issue areas such as just wars, distributive justice, and human rights. Rather my focus will be meta-theoretical or meta-ethical: What is the status of normative theorizing in the discipline? What kind of intellectual 'space' has the traditional positivist dominance of theorizing in the discipline left for normative theorizing? And what are the possibilities of theorizing ethical questions in world politics in terms of postmodern epistemologies and ontologies?

Secondly, I will address the question of critical theory's engagement in social criticism in relation to the 'practical political activity' in which a great many International Relations scholars are already involved: that of teaching world politics. Overall, however, the intent of this chapter parallels that of those which preceded it: to show how the predominance of positivism in social science has inhibited the development of theorizing which is self-consciously engaged in social criticism, and to show why positivism's influence can and must be challenged.

Value-freedom and International Relations theory

To begin, there is little question that the positivist quest for value-freedom has been a prominent fixture of contemporary theorizing about world politics. As Smith has noted,

> For the vast majority of students of International Relations educated during the 1950s, 1960s and 1970s, the dominance of positivism as an epistemological orthodoxy was obvious, so obvious that its assumptions were rarely questioned. Values and analysis had to be kept apart. The former could inform the analyst as citizen or,

possibly, determine what he or she looked at, but had to be omitted from the process of analysis itself.[3]

James Rosenau's admonition that 'To think theoretically one has to be clear as to whether one aspires to empirical theory or value theory' serves as a perfect example of the way positivist strictures have been applied to the study of world politics.[4] 'Progress in the study of international affairs', he argues,

> depends on advances in both empirical and value theory. But the two are not the same. They may overlap; they can focus on the same problem; and values always underlie the selection of the problems to which empirical theories are addressed. Yet they differ in one overriding way: empirical theory deals essentially with the 'is' of international phenomena, with things as they are if and when they are subjected to observation, while value theory deals essentially with the 'ought' of international phenomena, with things as they should be if and when they could be subjected to manipulation.[5]

Rosenau is willing to concede that the 'habit of making the necessary analytical, rhetorical, and evidential distinctions between empirical and value theory can be difficult' to develop.[6] 'Young students' and those 'who have strong value commitments and a deep concern for certain moral questions', notes Rosenau, are particularly susceptible to laxity in this regard.[7] He attempts to counter this tendency by assuring those with strong moral commitments that 'Empirical theory is not superior to moral theory; it is simply preferable for certain purposes, and one of these is the end of deepening our grasp of why international processes unfold as they do.'[8] Moreover, he argues,

> moral values and policy goals can be ... best served, by putting them aside and proceeding detachedly long enough to enlarge empirical understanding of the obstacles that hinder realization of the values and progress toward the goals.[9]

Rosenau also recognizes that 'impatience with [purely] empirical theorizing' tends to be 'especially intense among Third World students of International Relations':

> The newly developed consciousness of the long-standing injustices built into First World–Third World relationships, the lure of dependency theory, and perhaps a frustration over the central tendencies of social science in the First World have made Third World theorists particularly resistant to detached empirical theorizing.[10]

And it is noteworthy that Rosenau is not unaffected by this resistance:

> Their resistance gives a First World scholar pause: is his insistence on habituating oneself to the is–ought distinction yet another instance of false superiority, of projecting onto the developing world practices that have worked in industrial societies?[11]

However, while Rosenau concedes that 'Of late I have become keenly aware of the biases that may underlie my intellectual endeavours', he concludes by reaffirming his commitment to the separation of fact and value:

> In this particular instance ... I cannot even begin to break the habit. The relevance of the distinction strikes me as global, as independent of any national biases, as necessary to thinking theoretically wherever and whenever enlarged comprehension is sought.[12]

It is not hard to see how the dominance of positivism in International Relations, as in social science more generally, places severe limitations on the development of theory engaged in social criticism. As Bernstein has noted, for the researcher committed to scientific standards of investigation, 'the very idea of the theorist as a critic of society and politics is avoided or ruled out by "methodological prohibitions"'.[13]

Accordingly, if a space for social criticism is to be created within the discipline of International Relations, the positivist tenet of the 'value-free' nature of scientific knowledge must be challenged. The mounting of such a challenge will proceed by way of a critical examination of the underlying assumption of that tenet: the assumption that it is possible to separate fact from value. Simply put, it will be argued that the claim that it is possible to separate fact and value cannot be sustained. In order to substantiate this conclusion, I will focus on the most rigorous effort within social science to ensure the separation of fact and value: that of the positivist approach itself.

Positivism's hidden normative content

As a first step to calling into question the assumption that it is possible to separate fact and value, I will review a set of arguments advanced in support of that assumption by one of the discipline's most sophisticated advocates of the positivist approach: Michael

Nicholson.[14] Nicholson is an ideal figure to engage in this regard. He holds the rare distinction of having made respected contributions in both International Relations and social and political theory more generally. Furthermore, not only are his positivist convictions clearly in evidence in his recent work on world politics, he is one of the very few in the discipline who has offered an extended justification for adopting the positivist approach in the first place.[15]

To begin, it should be noted that Nicholson's commitment to the positivist tenet of value-freedom is closely tied to his acceptance of the accompanying positivist tenets of 'truth as correspondence' and the methodological unity of science. With regard to the former, he notes that it is a core requirement for science that propositions be formed which are both unambiguous (so as to be widely understood), and 'which are empirical in the sense that observations can confirm or refute them'.[16] And with regard to the second, he affirms that there

> does seem to me good reason to think that there can be explanation of social behaviour, and in particular political behaviour, which in style follows the general pattern of the explanation of natural phenomena.[17]

It is in his defence of the assumption that it is possible to separate fact and value, however, that Nicholson distinguishes himself. He begins by affirming that the question of whether the search for a value-free social science is itself misguided is wholly dependent upon the answer one gives to the question of whether 'explanation and evaluation can be separated in the social sciences'. Nicholson's answer is unambiguous: 'With qualifications', he affirms, 'I believe they can'.[18]

Unlike cruder advocates of positivism, Nicholson is more than willing to recognize that the activity of scientific research takes place in an environment in which values are ubiquitous. He is prepared to concede, moreover, that individual researchers who are committed to a positivist approach to the study of society may be influenced by their personal values in the pre-scientific choice of topic or research area. He also recognizes that the findings of scientific research may be applied in the post-research context in value-laden ways.

None of this, however, is taken to invalidate the goal of value-free knowledge. Indeed, it is because of his recognition of the ubiquitousness of values and norms that Nicholson lays such stress on a research methodology designed to prevent the incursion of extraneous values into the scientific research process itself.

The key to substantiating the possibility of distinguishing fact from value, argues Nicholson, is to grasp the 'simple distinction between the content of a statement and the act of asserting that statement'. He clarifies this distinction as follows:

> A set of statements can be in itself totally value-free, but their assertion in a certain context can be a moral act. For example, a lecture on how to kill someone with bare hands could consist entirely of factual statements to the effect that blows of a certain amount of force on specified parts of the anatomy will have specific effects on the 'recipient' ... It would scarcely be denied ... that to give such a lecture would be a moral act, however neutral its vocabulary or well-established its propositions.[19]

Even so, Nicholson reaffirms, 'the circumstances of a sentence's utterance ... must be scrupulously differentiated from the content of the sentence itself'.[20] It is the latter that imparts a normative dimension to the statements, and not the statements themselves. They remain, in and of themselves, value-free. Accordingly, Nicholson concludes, there is 'no excuse for muddling the moral and evaluative judgements with science itself. These are of a totally different character and non-scientific' – a judgment which, he stresses, should not be understood as 'pejorative'.[21]

Nicholson's defence of the positivist goal of value-freedom is all the more noteworthy in terms of the present discussion given that it is intended to refute the claims of radical critics:

> There is a widespread view that an empiricist social science of anything, but perhaps in particular international conflict, is fraudulent in its pretensions because social science is inherently a political activity and in fact tends to be in the service of the status quo.[22]

It is certainly the case, notes Nicholson, that

> inasmuch as one wants to alter society, then one does it by a knowledge or assumed knowledge of social behaviour which is parallel in general form to the scientific laws of the behaviour of inanimate material.[23]

However, he argues, the very neutrality of the statement of social laws means that the study of how they might be used to change society 'can be fruitfully studied by reactionary, conservative, reformist or revolutionary'.[24] The point is, in the end, quite simple: 'Why one wants to alter social behaviour is not a scientific question: how one alters behaviour is.'[25]

How, then, can Nicholson's conclusion be countered? Some of the evidence to support such an argument has already surfaced in preceding chapters. We need only review it quickly here. First, in our discussion of reflexivity, it was noted that the positivist limiting of reason to *episteme* has the effect of rendering problematic – if not foreclosing altogether – the application of reason to the realm of normative discourse. The direct result is that the adjudication of normative questions, being by definition of a 'non-scientific' character, becomes entirely derivative of a/non rational factors (i.e., 'personal' value preferences) located beyond the reach of reasoned debate or criticism.

Indeed, Frost has argued that the predominance of positivism in International Relations theory – in his terms, the 'positivist bias' – has resulted in the paucity of normative theorizing in the discipline. Frost links the 'positivist bias' (i.e., the equating of reason with *episteme*) to 'prevailing doubts about the worth of normative theory relating to International Relations generally'.[26] He notes further the resulting tendency to conceive of normative discourse in 'decisionistic' terms – as arationally (if not anti-rationally) 'emotivist' in nature, where

> a value judgement may be seen as purely arbitrary, i.e. it may be seen as a judgement for which a person simply opts [which] is neither right nor wrong, but is simply what the person has chosen.[27]

In short, there is no reason to doubt positivists such as Rosenau and Nicholson when they affirm their respect for non-scientific 'normative theory'. However, it must also be recognized that in a social and political context where reason is both privileged and limited to scientistic *episteme*, to term an issue area 'non-scientific' cannot but be pejorative in its effect. And given positivism's contribution to the making of that context, and thereby to the impoverishment of normative discourse, it must be concluded that positivist social science has a clear normative content *in and of itself*.

Similarly, in our discussion of the treatment of human consciousness it was noted that positivism's commitment to naturalism and the methodological unity of science has an undeniable normative dimension. The resulting reification of social facts and behavioural regularities sets clear limits on the scope of change deemed possible. It is in this sense that positivism can be understood to promote an accommodation to existing forms of life. It is also in this sense that it can be argued that positivism limits not only the scope of change possible, but also limits the task of theory to facilitating the functioning of the given order. Once again, any tradition which promotes 'wise resignation' in the face of 'what is' (i.e., behavioural regularities), and which actively contributes to the maintenance of the status quo, has a clear normative content *in and of itself*.

There is a third sense, however, in which it can be argued that the positivist approach has a clear normative content. In this case, positivism's normative content derives not from its impoverishment of normative discourse, nor from its tendency to reinforce existing forms of life, but from the kind of politics which derive from its conceptualization of the relation of theory to practice.

It will be remembered from the overview of the positivist tradition in chapter two that the structure of explanation is one in which there exists a symmetry between explanation of the occurrence of a phenomenon in the past and the prediction of the reoccurrence of that phenomenon in the future. That is, it is integral to positivism's structure of explanation that the subsumption of an occurrence under a general covering law – coupled with the assumption that such occurrences are manifestations of regularities independent of time and place – will allow for an exact determination of the conditions under which that phenomenon will reoccur.

It is this symmetry of explanation and prediction within the positivist tradition which provides the basis for manipulative control of the natural world. It is this symmetry of explanation and prediction which has led to the near-miraculous successes of natural science in areas as varied as the exploration of space and the splitting of the atom.

However, the significance of positivism's theory of explanation goes further. As Fay has noted, this theory of explanation is rooted in and expressive of 'a whole series of metaphysical assumptions as to the nature of truth and reality'.[28] That is, for the positivist-inspired researcher,

> reality is comprised of observable objects and events which are related nomologically, i.e. they are related according to a series of general laws of the type, if X then Y under situation C, and that therefore, in line with this scientific assumption about reality, only statements which reveal the concrete forms which those general relationships take can be true statements. Science must view the

world this way in order for it to provide the kind of explanations it prizes, which is to say, in order for it to provide the control over the phenomena which is a sign of its having understood a phenomenon. Because science marks out the 'world' as a world of observable phenomena subject to general laws it thereby is *constituting this 'world' from the viewpoint of how one can gain control over it.*[29]

Concludes Fay:

It is for this reason that possible technical control provides the framework within which the definition of reality and truth in [positivist] science occurs ... The possibility of controlling variables is a factor in terms of which one distinguishes a cognitive enterprise as scientific, and thus technical control is a defining element in the scientific enterprise itself.[30]

In short, the positivist conception of the relationship between theory and practice is one of knowledge of regularities for the purpose of exercising instrumental control.

It is important to note that the in-built interest in technical control which Fay identifies in the positivist theory of explanation is not limited to applications of the positivist approach to the natural world. In that the structure of explanation remains unchanged, it can be asserted that positivism's interest in control is equally present in its application to the study of the social world. Indeed, it is noteworthy that from the beginning, positivist theorists have been quite cognizant of and explicit about this interest. 'From Science comes Prevision', noted Comte, and 'from Prevision comes Control'.[31]

The conduct of scientific inquiry conceived as an interest in control in the social world has definite normative content. For the objects of technical control in the case of a 'science of society' are neither atoms nor molecules – they are human beings. As a consequence, the application of a positivist approach to the study of science cannot be separated from the form of politics implicit in the interest in the technical control of human beings integral to positivism's theory of explanation. Notes Marcuse:

The science of nature develops under the *technological a priori* which projects nature as potential instrumentality, stuff of control and organization. And the apprehension of nature as (hypothetical) instrumentality *precedes* the development of all particular technical organization ...

The technological *a priori* is a political *a priori* inasmuch as the transformation of nature involves that of man, and inasmuch as the 'man-made creations' issue from and re-enter a societal ensemble. One may still insist that the machinery of the technological universe is 'as such' indifferent towards political ends ... However, when technics becomes the universal form of material production, it circumscribes an entire culture; it projects a historical totality – a 'world'.[32]

In short, the form of politics which corresponds to positivist social science's interest in technical control is quite simply a politics of 'domination', in which 'Scientific–technical rationality and manipulation are welded together into new forms of social control.'[33] Within this form of politics, the manipulation of human behaviour and even human thought is key. Moreover, it is a defining characteristic of this form of politics that control is exercised over the majority by a small minority of 'technical experts', whose knowledge of the regularities manifest in the social world allows for the effective control of that world.

Of course, in liberal democratic societies, technical experts are nominally under the control of the elected representatives of the people at large. Yet as Habermas has noted, the politics of 'domination' – in his terms, the politics of 'technocratic consciousness' – are increasingly marked by a situation in which 'the objective necessity disclosed by the specialists seems to assert itself over the [elected] leaders' decisions':

> The dependence of the professional [technical expert] on the politician appears to have reversed itself. The latter becomes the mere agent of a scientific intelligentsia which, in concrete circumstances, elaborates the objective implications and requirements of available techniques and resources as well as of optimal strategies and rules of control ... The political would then be at best something of a stopgap in a still imperfect rationalization of power, in which the initiative in any case passed to scientific analysis and technical planning.[34]

As a consequence, concludes Marcuse, positivism's 'Technological rationality ... protects rather than cancels the legitimacy of domination, and the instrumentalist horizon of reason opens on a rationally totalitarian society.'[35]

This discussion has direct relevance for an assessment of the normative content of positivist theorizing about world politics. It is significant that Nicholson promotes the adoption of a scientific approach to the study of world politics because 'our ability to understand and control social systems is low'.[36] On the other hand, he argues, 'the firmer is our knowledge of social behaviour, the greater our potential control over it';[37] the more extensive our grasp of the social laws and regularities, the greater our ability to engage in 'social engineering' in the interest of human betterment.[38]

There is no need to question Nicholson's motives in this regard. His genuine concern with finding solutions to humanity's pressing problems (e.g., war) is obvious. Nor is he incorrect in his assertion that the study of how social laws might be used to change society 'can be fruitfully studied by reactionary, conservative, reformist or revolutionary'. Where he is wrong is in assuming that the positivist-inspired social engineering he advocates is neutral with regard to the implementation of a particular political programme. What I have endeavoured to show here is that positivist social engineering has its own *telos* which will necessarily inform the kind of political practices that result from its adoption as the strategy for social change.

The nature of positivism's hidden normative content is now manifest. In its contribution to the impoverishment of discourse about normative issues, in its reification of social practices, and finally, in its very promotion of a politics of domination, the positivist approach to the study of the social world cannot be seen as 'value-free'. In short, and '[d]espite all the talk of objectivity and value neutrality', it is clear that positivist social science – including positivist International Relations theory – is 'shot through with explicit and implicit value judgements, and controversial normative and ideological claims'.[39]

What conclusions may be drawn from this discussion? In fact, the implications are more far reaching than simply concluding that positivist knowledge has undeniable normative content. We have already noted that positivism has made a concerted and on-going effort to separate fact from value in the production of 'value-free' scientific knowledge. If positivism has failed in that effort, then it is reasonable to conclude that the very assumption of the possibility of separating fact and value must itself be reconsidered; the very tenet of 'value-freedom' in scientific knowledge reassessed.

In short, what positivism's failure to separate fact from value shows is that the goal of 'value-freedom' in scientific knowledge is a chimera. Accordingly, the proper question is not 'How can normative concerns be accommodated within the value-free scientific enterprise?', but rather, 'What norms and values inform what kinds of theorizing?'

Recognizing positivist International Relations theory's hidden normative content allows us to understand the significance of recent developments in the discipline for the restructuring of International Relations theory. With regard to positivism's contribution to a politics of domination, for example, one notes the growing concern with the dangers posed by the 'scientization of politics'. Ashley, for example, has criticized positivist neorealism's reduction of politics to 'pure technique': 'Political strategy is deprived of its artful and performative aspect, becoming instead the mere calculation of instruments of control.'[40]

The undemocratic implications are clear:

> Absent from neorealist categories is any hint of politics as a creative, critical enterprise, an enterprise by which men and women might reflect on their goals and strive to shape freely their collective will.[41]

In short, concludes Ashley, positivist neorealism is 'an ideology that anticipates, legitimizes, and orients a *totalitarian project* of global proportions'.[42]

A similar recognition of positivism's normative content in terms of its reification of social relations underlies the growing calls for theorizing which stresses 'interpretation, practice, and the *critique of reification*',[43] and which shows itself willing to stand 'apart from the prevailing order of the world and ask[ ] how that order came about', in order that it might 'clarify [the] range of possible alternatives' to the existing order, and in this way serve as 'a guide to strategic action for bringing about an alternative order'.[44]

Perhaps the greatest significance of the present discussion, however, lies in the space such a recognition creates for explicitly normative theorizing in the discipline. It is to a consideration of this issue that we now turn.

The resurgence of normative International Relations theory

As has already been noted, positivism's equating of reason with *episteme* lay at the root of 'prevailing doubts about the worth of normative theory relating to International Relations generally'.[45] Accordingly, the explicit rejection of the 'decisionist' implications of positivism's conception of truth as correspondence to the facts implicit in recent efforts in normative International Relations theory is a welcome development.[46] In a clear break with positivism's limiting of reason to *episteme*, recent contributions in normative International Relations theory have reaffirmed the possibility of rational debate about normative issues and the integration of such debates into the theory process.

At the same time, however, there are problems attached to the renewed interest in normative International Relations theory. The first is that in attempting to establish the legitimacy of explicitly normative theory, there is a temptation to revert to the problematic notion of two types of theorizing, one of which is 'normative' and the other 'non-normative'. This is a strategy adopted by Chris Brown in his recent work on normative theory.[47] Significantly, Brown poses a question virtually identical to that posed by Nicholson. 'Is it, in fact, possible', he asks, 'to have theory that is not in some sense concerned with the business of standard setting and norm creating?' Equally significantly, Brown's answer also parallels that of Nicholson: 'Rhetoric aside, yes, it is possible to have that kind of theory.'[48]

Taken literally, of course, Brown is correct. It is indeed possible to have theory that is not *concerned* with the business of standard setting and norm creating. But that it is possible to have theory that is not, in actuality, setting standards and creating norms is an entirely different question, and one which, on the basis of our discussion of positivism's hidden normative content, would have to be answered in the negative. In short, the liability inherent in the representation of normative International Relations theory as the twin to 'non-normative' theory is that it reinforces the legitimacy of the positivist tenet of value-freedom, and thereby of the hegemony of positivism itself.

A second problem with recent efforts in normative International Relations theory is the failure to challenge adequately the positivist accommodation of 'normative' to 'non-normative theory'.[49] For positivists, the need for normative theory is tied directly to the successful development of empirical accounts: in the words of Michael Nicholson, the greater our potential control over social behaviour, 'the greater the need for clarification of moral issues'.[50] In a context in which positivist conceptions retain great influence, the consequences of not challenging those conceptions are extremely serious. What is required in the present context is not simply a greater concern with normative issues, but rather the recognition that the study of world politics is, and always has been, unavoidably normative; not that normative concerns ought to be addressed, but that 'they have always been at the centre of the subject'; that

> Lying at the heart of value-neutrality was a very powerful normative project, one every bit as 'political' or 'biased' as those approaches marginalized and delegitimized in the name of science.[51]

It is in this regard that normative International Relations theory can make a significant contribution. It is also in this regard that the positivist conception of the proper relation of normative to 'non-normative' theory poses such a danger. Simply put, unless the positivist conception of the relationship of 'normative' to 'non-normative' theory is countered, the renewed interest in normative International Relations theory may end up providing little more than clarification on the potential ends to which a politics of domination may be put – a form of theory limited to dealing 'with things as they should be *if and when they could be subjected to manipulation'*.[52]

It might, of course, be countered that the continuing centrality of problematic positivist concerns and categories in recent explorations of normative International Relations theory is simply a reflection of the fact that much of the discussion of ethics and world politics is being conducted in decidedly *modernist* terms. If true, then recent efforts to elucidate a postmodern view of ethics and world politics must be considered as well. To begin, there is no question that postmodernist International Relations theorists have made ethics a central concern. David Campbell's *Politics Without Principle: Sovereignty, Ethics and the Narratives of the Gulf War*, for example, makes a significant contribution in this regard.[53] Inspired by the Foucaultian notion that 'war is the narration of politics/the political by other means',[54] Campbell draws upon postmodern 'discourse analysis' to analyse the discursive practices that moved the crisis toward conflict - in particular, the 'discourse of moral certitude' through which the West attributed all responsibility for the war to Iraq.

What is arguably most significant is Campbell's attempt in the final chapter of the book to 'articulate an ethico-political disposition that is both consonant with the complexities of the postmodern world and capable of encouraging us to resist undemocratic practices'.[55] The elements of the ethico-political disposition Campbell promotes are as follows. First, it is necessary to recognize that the notion of the 'autonomous subject' cannot be sustained; that subjects are constituted intersubjectively – that is, 'by their relationship with the Other'.[56] Following from this is the recasting of the notion of ethics from one of 'a set of rules and regulations adopted by autonomous agents – to something insinuated within and integral to that subjectivity'.[57] Accordingly, argues Campbell,

> ethics is not ancillary to the existence of a subject ...; ethics is indispensable to the very being of that subject, because a subject's being is only possible once its *right to be* in relation to the Other is claimed.[58]

The consequence of this is the recognition

> that 'we' are always already ethically situated; making judgments about conduct, therefore, depends less on what sort of rules are invoked as regulations [morality], and more on how the interdependencies of our relations with others are appreciated.[59]

Accordingly, ethics is recast from efforts to derive objectively valid general(izable) rules of social behaviour to a recognition and acceptance of 'heteronomous responsibility'.[60]

The significance of such a shift in the view of the subject and of ethics, argues Campbell, is the way it would alter standard practices in international politics. Were such a view of the subject and ethics to be embraced in foreign policy, for example, the result would be a greater 'appreciation for ambiguity and a sensitivity to contingency' the result of which would be that 'the adversarial or the unexpected [would] not become an occasion for moral absolutism and violent retribution akin to the dark days of the Cold War'.[61] In the face of growing interdependence, such a disposition counsels 'humility rather than hubris', an engagement with the world that 'seeks to affirm life', and, as a consequence, 'might offer the prospect of an improved quality of life for many'.[62]

Campbell's intervention is to be welcomed; his efforts to elucidate a life-affirming ethics is certainly consistent with the general thrust of the present study. Nor is he alone in this regard. Framing their theorizing in terms of an 'ethics of freedom', Ashley and Walker define the goal of postmodern International Relations theorizing as that of aiding persons occupying 'marginal sites'[63] to

> proceed in a register of freedom to explore and test institutional limitations in a way that sustains and expands the cultural spaces and resources enabling one to conduct one's labours of self-making

in just this register of freedom, further exploring and testing limitations.[64]

In this regard, Walker's championing of a 'postmodern politics of resistance' bears noting.[65] Walker directs attention to the struggles of 'critical social movements': movements, in the North and in the South engaged with a multitude of issues; movements whose members are

> suspicious of all Traditional claims for emancipation on behalf of *the* people, *the* class, *the* common interest and sceptical of all singular, homogenized images of 'reality,' 'liberty,' 'freedom,' and all 'isms' proclaiming post-Enlightenment visions of *the* good life;[66]

movements that seek to 'extend processes of democratization into realms where it has never been tried: into the home, into the workplace, into processes of cultural production'.[67]

How, then, are we to assess postmodern interventions on the question of ethics? Not surprisingly, this is not a simple matter. On the one hand, it is clear that the emphasis on pluralism and the diversity of experience and identity, and on the need to hear the voices of the marginalized, is an important corrective to modernity's 'monologic' tendencies. In this, postmodern International Relations theorists represent the best of postmodernism generally: that is, the sensitivity

> to the multifarious ways in which the 'history of the West' – even in its institutionalization of communicative practices – has always tended to silence differences, to exclude outsiders and exiles, those who live on the margins.[68]

Still, as valuable and important as these postmodern interventions are, there are serious questions that pose themselves. The first is that of the question of human agency or subjectivity. In simplest terms, it is not always clear if postmodernism rejects only the traditional notion of a fully formed subject – the *cogito* of Western philosophy – or whether its rejection encompasses the notion of subjectivity *tout court*. And as has been observed in relation to Foucault's aestheticized conception of ethics – ethics defined as treating one's life as a 'work of art' – it is uncertain that the line remains uncrossed. As Bernstein notes, one of the more problematic issues

> is [that] the very way in which Foucault talks about ethics in terms of the self's relationship to itself *seems* to presuppose a way of speaking about the self that he had previously so effectively

criticized. What precisely is a 'self'? How is the 'self' related to what Foucault calls a 'subject'? Who is the 'I' that constitutes 'itself' as a moral agent?[69]

Parallel questions can be raised about postmodern International Relations. If we follow Ashley in adopting a Foucaultian-derived genealogical attitude which

> accounts for the constitution of knowledges, discourses, domains of objects, etc. *without having to refer to a subject*, whether it be transcendental in relation to the field of events or whether it chase its empty identity throughout history ...[70]

then who is the subject who constitutes itself in relation to the Other? If we accept the genealogical standpoint that

> there are no subjects ... having an existence prior to practice ... [that] the subject is itself a site of power political contest, and ceaselessly so ... [that] the subject itself exists as an identifiable subject only in the precarious balancing and dispersal of plural interpretive elements resulting from the continuing strategic inter-play of multiple alien forms ...[71]

then who is it that is to 'conduct one's labours of self-making' in a register of freedom?

If, on the other hand, the point of postmodernism is not to deny subjectivity in its entirety, but only the notion of a fully formed, atomistic subject, we are confronted with the question of the relation-ship of the postmodern version of the subject to that of modernist theorizing. Campbell is surely right in saying that within the modernist metaphysical tradition (and the conventional International Relations literature it informs) subjectivity is often understood as autonomous agency, and ethics as a set of objectively grounded 'rules of conduct or the moral code that undergirds, through various commands, the path to the good and just life';[72] that the dominant model of ethics within modernist theorizing rests upon the notion 'of a deep self, a hidden other, for example the unconscious or the real me, that is the location of some constellation of one's real interests, beliefs, feelings, or concerns'.[73] It is this model of subjectivity and ethics which is the proper object of Campbell's critique.

Yet it must also be stressed that modernist theorizing is not a monolith. Specifically, it is not necessary to abandon modernist theorizing to encounter the recognition of the 'relational character of subjectivity' or the conception of ethics as context-dependent reflection on deeply contrastable ways of being in the world. These elements are also present within the 'critical–expressivist' approach to ethics.[74] Here the notion of the subject is one in which desires, beliefs, and feelings are located between two poles:

> On the one hand, there are those desires, beliefs, and feelings that I reflectively choose and (more or less) understand the conditions of their existence or emergence. On the other hand, there are those desires, beliefs, and feelings that are formed under mistaken assumptions, tied to wrong objects, or are the result, in some mechanical sense, of external effects.[75]

Furthermore, the critical–expressivist model directs us to radically different questions from the dominant approach to ethics. Instead of the correspondence-oriented query of 'How am I able to get my conscious self, interests, ideas, etc. to correspond to or represent my real interests?', the questions that emerge are those that seem quite in harmony with the kind of reoriented ethical reflection Campbell wishes to promote, namely:

> How have I come to have the feelings, desires, and interests that I have? Are they the types of feelings, etc., that I want to have, given the opportunity to choose between alternatives, or are they the outcome of some previously unrecognized processes of which I have little or no control?[76]

However, it is not simply that it is possible to explore the intersubjective constitution of the subject from within modernist theorizing. The point is that it may be difficult to do so adequately from anywhere but within modernity. For to be concerned with the kind of ethical reflection desired by both Campbell and critical-expressivism is, as Gibbons has argued,

> to be concerned with the conditions under which one can more easily engage in this type of reflection and, subsequently, to be concerned with the conditions under which critical reflection flourishes. This in turn leads one to consider the social and political arrangements that encourage that type of reflection and allows the questions of political reflection and the problems of political philosophy to emerge.[77]

In this way we are brought to a second problem-area with regard to postmodern discussions of ethics – that of the unwillingness to provide a conception of the 'good' having pretensions to universalizability. Specifically, what is at issue here is the postmodernist

resistance to specifying what kinds of social and political arrange-
ments are conducive to the 'good life', and what kinds of action
strategies are best suited for achieving that life.

The postmodernist unease with defining the good in abstraction is
not difficult to find in the writings of postmodern International
Relations theorists. In the words of Ashley and Walker,

> we cannot represent, formalize, or maxim-ize deterritorialized
> modalities of ethical conduct. We cannot evoke a juridical model,
> define the good life and lay down the code crucial to its fulfilment,
> as if bespeaking some universal consensus formed according to rules
> of discourse already given, without at the same time covertly
> imposing a principle of territoriality that these modalities refuse to
> entertain.[78]

Likewise, Campbell's treatment of the Gulf War is very much in
keeping with the postmodernist disinclination to define the good or
the means to achieve it: tellingly, he gives scant attention to the issue
of how political structures and power relations – domestically and
globally – would have to change for a view of ethics as 'heteronomous responsibility' to become the guiding framework for policy-
making. Nor does Campbell suggest which social forces might lead in
the struggle to effect those far-reaching changes. Similarly, statements
such as 'Poststructuralism [postmodernism] ... is an emphatically
political perspective' but one 'which refuses to privilege any partisan
political line'[79] are reflective of that resistance.

Postmodernists are quick to insist, moreover, that an unwillingness
to define the good does not preclude a discussion of normative issues
in their theorizing. In the words of Ashley and Walker,

> our inability to represent human beings does not prevent us from
> talking about it [the good life] or from trying to understand how it
> might orient deterritorialized ethics in the valuation and disciplining
> of their activities.[80]

There are, however, problems associated with the postmodern
position. To begin, is it really correct to say, as postmodernists seem
to do, that the effort to give substantive content to the notion of the
'good life', or to action strategies designed to achieve it, must
inevitably bespeak 'some universal consensus formed according to
rules of discourse already given'? Hermeneutically oriented theorists
have argued, to the contrary, that much is to be gained, even in the
absence of universal consensus or pre-given rules of discourse,

through the 'joining of horizons' of different notions of the good and of the traditions in which those notions are embedded.[81]

Furthermore, it can be argued that the postmodern position entails serious liabilities in terms of the exercise of ethical judgment necessary to emancipatory solidarity. Once again, a parallel can be drawn between postmodern International Relations and postmodernism more generally. Foucault's championing of an 'insurrection of subjugated knowledges' of those on the margins of history has provoked concerns about how one is to engage in critical assessment of those knowledges. As Bernstein notes, not unsympathetically,

> if we stick to the specific and local – to the *insurrection of subjected knowledges* – there is an implicit valorization here that never quite becomes fully explicit, and yet is crucial for Foucault's genre of critique. For there are subjected knowledges of women, Blacks, prisoners, gays, who have experienced the pain and suffering of exclusion. But throughout the world there are also the subjected knowledges of all sorts of fundamentalists, fanatics, terrorists, who have their own sense of what are the unique or most important dangers to be confronted. What is never quite clear in Foucault is why anyone should favor certain local forms of resistance rather than others. Nor is it clear why one would 'choose' one side or the other in a localized resistance or revolt.[82]

Similar questions can be posed to postmodern International Relations. For example, serious scrutiny is warranted by Bradley Klein's affirmation that the proper task of a post-hegemonic (i.e., postmodern) study of world politics is to

> ask interesting questions that speak to, and listen to, ongoing social and political struggles. In this sense, the task of social science is to give voice and clarity to the multiple forces and social movements that help constitute world politics.[83]

The problem with this position is obvious: in limiting itself to a neutral, non-partisan representation of contending voices, it fails to take a position on the respective merits and liabilities of the differing political and social agendas being pursued by the 'multiple forces and social movements that help constitute world politics'. At the same time, however, in the absence of a notion of the 'good life', it is unclear that postmodern International Relations can aspire to anything more than a non-judgmental representation.

Similar concerns can be raised about Walker's support for critical social movements in their struggle for democracy. Walker's resistance to specifying universalizable notions of justice is clearly manifest in his statement that 'Universalism, to put it bluntly and heretically, can be understood as the problem, not the solution.'[84] In the absence of a conception of the 'good' with pretensions to universalizability, however, how is one to know which social movements are truly 'critical' and which are reactionary?; in the absence of a discussion of the 'good life', how is one to know what constitutes real democracy and what is merely a deformed caricature thereof?

Significantly, in his earlier work Walker acknowledges this dilemma, wishing, as he does, to distinguish progressive 'critical' social movements from their 'reactionary' authoritarian counterparts:

> Whether as Klu Klux Klan, as religious fundamentalisms, or through slogans about evil empires and the magic of the market, the reactionary forces of our time maximize exclusion, render complexities in sharp strokes of black and white, and reject connections in favor of keeping their backs to the wall and their weapons out ... whatever the populist or democratic rhetoric, movements of reaction exaggerate hierarchies and justify the need for order from above. These forces of reaction are profoundly antidemocratic.[85]

Such a vigorous (and welcome) condemnation of the forces of reaction is only possible, however, on the basis of universalizable notions of the value of democracy, equality, and solidarity with others pursuing emancipatory aims. It is surely significant, moreover, that in this context – and in contrast to his pronouncements in others – Walker concedes that:

> The problem is not the claims of universalism as such ... [but] rather, the way in which universalism has come to be framed as both the opposite of and superior to pluralism and difference.[86]

Such a concession, however, raises once again the question of the relation of postmodern to modernist theorizing. If the goal of postmodernist theorizing is not to reject universalism, but rather to reconcile some form of universalism with a respect for pluralism and difference, then what distinguishes those efforts from modernist ones?[87]

In the end, the resistance of postmodernists to defining the 'good life' is not difficult to locate: the question of the political arrangements that encourage ethical behaviour, after all, 'constitute the ethos of the Enlightenment and modernity';[88] at the same time, these are issues which postmodernists have decried as being constitutive of the discourse of 'governability, sovereignty and discipline' – the themes that typify political thought and action in the modern, carceral society.[89]

It would seem, however, that universalizable conceptions of the good life – and of the means to achieve it that are consistent with the ends pursued – are not merely useful, they are indispensable. They are indispensable if we are to choose wisely, to act justly, and to work in solidarity with others for emancipatory ends. Accordingly, it is not at all clear that postmodern International Relations theorists can find a way to avoid being drawn back into some version of *modern* social and political theory if they pursue an 'engagement with the world' that 'seeks to affirm life' by means of an 'ethic of freedom' to its logical conclusion.

Critical restructuring and emancipatory pedagogy

There are two reasons why taking up the issue of pedagogy is a fitting way to conclude this chapter. To begin, the positivist 'logic of investigation' had strong implications not only for research but for pedagogy as well. Specifically, the tenet of value-freedom posited a strict separation of facts and values not only in the process of analysis, but also in the practice of teaching. As such, the role of the teacher was largely limited to that of representing, in a neutral, objective fashion, the 'facts' of world politics, devoid of any normative assessment. Certainly, the proper task of the teacher was not to promote a specific value orientation in the classroom, but rather to help students internalize a positivist orientation to values.

Of course, total success in this regard was never guaranteed. As Rosenau has noted, with discernible frustration,

> I have found that helping students become habituated to the is–ought distinction is among the most difficult pedagogical tasks. They can understand the distinction intellectually and they can even explain and defend it when pressed; but practising it is another matter.[90]

Still, the goal of responsible teaching was clear.

It is surely significant, in light of the concerns of this chapter, that the renewed interest in normative International Relations theory has been paralleled by increasing attentiveness to the question of 'engaged pedagogy'. A recent volume of contributions on the topic of teaching world politics, for example, frames the question of pedagogy in terms of an unambiguous commitment to 'reducing the inherited tension between justice, peace, and security',[91] by (re)presenting the world to students not as a 'given' to be accepted, but as a 'world of our making'[92] which can, in principle, be remade.

The explicit commitment to an 'engaged pedagogy' – that is, a pedagogy rooted in a self-conscious commitment to criticizing the status quo in the interests of justice and peace – is certainly a welcome one. The activity of teaching affords a clear opportunity for engaging in social criticism in support of the transformation of established 'forms of life'.

It can be argued, however, that while the politico-normative impetus to teaching is crucial, what has not received sufficient attention in regard to 'engaged pedagogy' is the way specific pedagogical strategies can serve either to support or undermine the commitments which give rise to teaching; the way they can, independently of the value commitments of the teacher, serve to promote either a politics of emancipation or, indeed, of domination.

This leads, then, to the second reason that the issue of pedagogy is important in this context. For critically oriented social theorists have argued that in the effort to 'be a guide to strategic action for bringing about an alternative order', emancipatory theorizing must incorporate an 'educative' – as opposed to an 'instrumental' – conception of that relationship. What is distinctive about an educative form of practice is that it

> does not see social theory as useful because it allows people to manipulate causal variables so that they can get what they want in an efficient manner. Instead, social theory is seen as a means by which people can achieve a much clearer picture of who they are, and of what the real meaning of their social practices is, as a first step in becoming different sorts of people with different sorts of social arrangements ... The purpose of ... theory is to engender self-knowledge and so to liberate people from the oppressiveness of their social arrangements.[93]

In short, an educative conception of the relationship between theory and practice corresponds not to the positivist goal of the replacement of politics by the 'administration of things', but to the democratic ideal of human beings consciously acting together to define and organize the community in which they live; not to the positivist *telos* of 'social engineering', but to the Aristotelian *telos* of the 'leading of a good and just life in the *polis*'.[94]

As a way of showing the importance of considering both the form and content of our pedagogical practices, I will draw on the work of Paulo Freire[95] to examine two strategies which can be used to address the central challenge for anyone teaching world politics: that of making global structures and processes, which almost inevitably appear distant and abstract, real and meaningful to students.

One popular strategy to meet that challenge is that of 'making the local, global'. By this I mean efforts by the teacher to bring the realities of global-level structures, processes and actors into the localized experiences of students in the classroom.[96] The underlying assumption of this strategy is that understanding international politics is a matter of acquiring a body of relatively unproblematic factual knowledge. If students are not in a position to understand the realm of international politics, it is simply a function of the fact that they lack that knowledge. Indeed, it is commonly noted, with considerable frustration, that students regularly lack even the most basic background knowledge about the world (i.e., the fundamentals of geography, history, etc.) thereby rendering the task of imparting the more specialized knowledge of world politics extremely difficult. The operative question then becomes, 'Given the widespread ignorance of the students we confront, which pedagogical techniques can be used to 'engineer' a learning context in which students will receive the knowledge required in the limited time available?'

The assumption and general thrust of the strategy of 'making the local, global' conform very closely to what Freire has termed 'banking education'. That is, education in which learning is understood as an apolitical process in which a body of neutral, objective information is 'deposited' in the students' minds where it can be retrieved later upon demand. In the words of Freire,

> In the banking concept of education, knowledge is a gift bestowed by those who consider themselves knowledgeable upon those whom they consider to know nothing.[97]

The assumption of absolute ignorance on the part of those to be taught is not a neutral one. In making this assumption, argues Freire, 'banking' education draws a distinction between teacher and student in a way that 'mirror[s] oppressive society as a whole'.[98] In the following list of the defining characteristics of the 'banking model',

Freire underscores how the relationship of teacher to student is reflected and reproduced:

> The teacher teaches and the students are taught.
> The teacher knows everything and the students know nothing.
> The teacher thinks and the students are thought about.
> The teacher talks and the students listen – meekly ...
> The teacher acts and the students have the illusion of acting through the action of the teacher.
> The teacher confuses the authority of knowledge with his own professional authority ...
> The teacher is the Subject of the learning process, while the students are mere objects.[99]

It should be noted that what is at issue here is the logic of the pedagogical practices in question, and not simply the aims of teachers. As Freire notes, certainly 'there are innumerable well-intentioned bank-clerk teachers who do not realize that they are serving only to dehumanize'.[100] Nonetheless, the politics of the pedagogical strategy informing the 'banking' model may overwhelm even the most admirable goals of the educator. In short, regardless of whether the intent is to promote social change or even just to 'educate', the pedagogical methodology employed has the effect of inculcating a world view that maintains relations of inequality and subordination, and contributes to a 'praxis of domination' in which people are rendered ever more vulnerable to control from above.

The intent of emancipatory theorizing, however, is surely the exact opposite: to shed light on the nature of relations of subordination and domination, and to work to 'demystify as ideological rival approaches that obfuscate[ ] or rationalize[ ] those relations'.[101] What kind of pedagogy is consistent with such an emancipatory intent?

Freire's counter-pedagogy is one which is fundamentally dialogical. It begins with the recognition that 'Teachers and students ... are both Subjects, not only in the task of unveiling ... reality, and thereby coming to know it critically, but in the task of re-creating that knowledge.'[102] To facilitate this dialogue between Subjects, teachers must begin with the understanding that students are not ignorant, empty vessels to be filled with objective knowledge, but rather self-reflecting and knowledgeable beings whose self-definitions and understandings must form the starting-point – though clearly not the end-point – of the learning process. Only by according recognition and respect to the knowledge that students bring with them can a meaningful dialogue be started. Only by affirming students in their identities as co-makers of the world they inhabit can the process of strategizing about remaking the world in a way consistent with emancipatory ends be initiated.

If the pedagogical strategy of 'making the local, global' conforms to that approach which Freire has named the 'banking' model of education, what strategy in the teaching of world politics would be consistent with his pedagogical alternative? That alternative strategy, drawing on the feminist insight that the 'personal is international',[103] can be termed 'making the global, local'. This second strategy entails identifying within the experiences and knowledge students bring with them to the classroom the presence of the global structures and processes which, at first encounter, seem so distant and abstract.

By way of example, the strategy of 'making the global, local' could involve drawing links between (i) male domination of classroom discussion time (statistically, men are much more likely to interrupt women than the inverse)[104] with global structures of patriarchy (e.g., 'women do 60 per cent of the world's work, make 10 per cent of the world's income, own 1 per cent of the world's property'); (ii) the great numbers of foreign nannies, on the one hand, and global economic processes such as IMF austerity programmes which underlie the Third World's export of women to work as servants for wealthy Northern families, on the other;[105] (iii) racist images and statements evident in popular culture (television situation comedies, rock videos) and racist colonialist and neo-colonialist foreign policies; and (iv) the high-priced, fashionable footwear that is *de rigueur* on so many campuses and the working conditions of Third World labourers engaged by transnational corporations in Export Processing Zones.

Like its counterpart, the strategy of 'making the global, local' is an effective means of making world politics real and meaningful. Furthermore, it has the added benefit of counterposing to the traditional view of world politics – that is, a political realm constituted by and consisting of the activities of state-elites – a vision which makes the activities and experiences of 'ordinary' non-elites as important in the production and reproduction of the global order as any other, thereby opening a space for theorizing strategies for changing the global order. And, last but not least, it stands in clear opposition to a politics of domination by affirming students as active agents of their own learning. In this way, the pedagogical strategy of 'making the global, local' helps to ensure that the results of an 'engaged pedagogy' are consistent with the politico-normative commitments which give rise to it.

Conclusion

The recognition of the implicit 'normative content' of positivist International Relations theory – and of the impossibility of 'value-free' knowledge – has important consequences in terms of the restructuring process which has served as the focus of this study. In general terms, it has helped to create a theoretical 'space' in the discipline of International Relations for self-consciously normative criticism of the established global order and the promotion of alternatives in both theory and practice. Finally, it has contributed to a growing consciousness on the part of International Relations scholars that their role as teachers must be framed in accordance with the need for 'transformative intellectuals' operating in the emancipatory interest.[106] As such, it stands as one more piece of evidence in support of the fundamental 'restructuring' of International Relations theory.

6 Conclusion

A political science which is true to its moral commitment ought at the very least to be an unpopular undertaking. At its very best, it cannot help being a subversive and revolutionary force with regard to certain vested interests – intellectual, political, economic, social in general.   Hans J. Morgenthau[1]

The value of a theory is not decided alone by the formal criteria of truth ... the value of a theory is decided by its connection with the tasks, which in the particular historical moment are taken up by *progressive social forces*.   Max Horkheimer[2]

This study has concerned itself with providing an answer to a very specific question: why is it that theory oriented toward human emancipation remains poorly developed within the discipline of International Relations? We are now in a position to provide an answer to this question, both in terms of what does explain the traditional absence of emancipatory International Relations theory as well as what does not.

This absence cannot be explained by either a lack of commitment to the improvement of human welfare on the part of International Relations theorists, or a lack of awareness by these theorists as to the nature of the threats under which our planet is living. Indeed, as was shown early on in this study, an explicit concern with human welfare is clearly manifest among a significant number of International Relations theorists. Though working out of different analytical traditions, these theorists remain united in their view of the study of

International Relations as 'the art and science of the survival of [human]kind'.[3]

This being the case, it was necessary to locate the explanation for the dearth of emancipatory theorizing elsewhere than the personal concern (or, rather, presumed lack of it) with the 'common good'. As a consequence, the explanation for the lack of emancipatory theorizing was sought in the very structure of mainstream International Relations theory. To do this, however, it was necessary to move beyond the bounds of International Relations theory proper, to avail ourselves of the insights of social and political theory more generally.

By drawing on a range of arguments put forward by social and political theorists, it was possible to arrive at an explanation of the virtual absence of emancipatory theory in terms of the predominance of the positivist approach in the discipline of International Relations. Specifically, the three tenets which together comprise the 'positivist logic of investigation' – that of 'truth as correspondence', the methodological unity of science, and the 'value-free' nature of scientific knowledge – were shown, in their turn, to have inhibited the development of the three elements which characterize emancipatory theory: 'theoretical reflexivity', attention to the active and creative role of human consciousness, and social criticism in support of the transformation of established 'forms of life'.

The benefits of the incorporation of the insights of social and political theory into a discussion of International Relations theory proved even more far-reaching than expected, however. For the insights afforded by social and political theory allowed for much more than a 'wrecking operation' in terms of positivist International Relations theory. Along with exposing the limitations of positivist International Relations theory – the non-viability of the separation of subject and object, naturalism, and the separation of fact and value – these insights also directed us toward positive alternatives for changing International Relations theory in a way more in harmony with the emancipatory imperative of the 'Aristotelian project'. Moreover, and perhaps most importantly, the meta-theoretical perspective afforded by social and political theory has also made clear the degree to which theorizing about international politics is already showing signs of undergoing such change – a 'restructuring' of International Relations theory. Specifically, it has become clear that in important respects International Relations theory already *is* being restructured in a post-positivist direction which is (i) self-consciously reflexive, (ii) intentionally interpretive, and (iii) explicitly critical of the existing global order. In short, the 'restructuring' of International Relations theory is its transformation into emancipatory, 'critical' theory.

Of course, noting the existence of critically oriented theorizing in the discipline can be no more than a starting-point. Crucial is the validation of that theorizing. And here, it bears noting that as a form of 'critical' theorizing, critical International Relations theory must be validated on two distinct levels. At one level, it must, like conventional forms of theorizing, be validated by developing reasoned arguments in support of its claims which are successful in gaining the assent of the relevant academic community. Yet while this level of validation is crucial, it is not sufficient. In the words of Horkheimer:

> General criteria for assessing critical theory as a whole do not exist, for they are always based on the recurrence of events and thus on a self-reproducing totality ... For all its insight into isolated events and for all the agreements of its elements with the most advanced traditional theories, critical theory has no specific authority on its side other than the interest in the abolition of social injustice which is connected to it.[4]

In short, a 'critical' International Relations theory must also validate itself in terms of the lives of those to whom it is ultimately directed.[5] Critical International Relations theory must realize itself in the concrete emancipation of human beings.

Of course, the appropriation of specific forms of theorizing never occurs in a vacuum. Currently, in the face of the limitations on the well-being and autonomy of the members of the global *polis* identified in the first chapter – limitations posed by weapons of mass destruction, the ecological crisis, the systematic violation of human rights around the globe, and the growing disparity between rich and poor within an increasingly interdependent world economy – people have increasingly begun to search for a global perspective to guide them in their locally based activities of organizing and resistance. In concrete terms, as the urban poor in underdeveloped countries have become increasingly aware that decisions made in International Monetary Fund boardrooms in Washington, DC have a profound impact on their daily struggle for survival, as workers in advanced industrial states have become increasingly conscious of the fact that the 'globalization' of national economies has a direct bearing on job security and living standards, as peace, human rights, and environ-

mental activists around the planet have become increasingly cognizant that militarization, environmental degradation, and human
rights violations are inextricably linked to existing global structures,
the demand for critical, emancipatory theory which incorporates a
global perspective has grown in stride. It is this demand, emanating
from a growing transnational constituency, for critical, emancipatory
theory with a global perspective which provides the emerging critical
International Relations theory identified in this study with a concrete
opportunity to realize itself – an opportunity which may well not
have existed even twenty years ago.

At the same time, this opportunity also draws our attention to the
limits of the restructuring process that has been identified. For while
it can be argued that significant changes are taking place at a *meta-
theoretical level*, it must also be recognized that those changes have
yet to be translated into significant gains in *theoretical–empirical* terms.
The enterprise of erecting substantive analyses of, for example, inter-
state conflict or global economic disparities upon the meta-theoretical
foundation of critical theory has hardly begun. In short, while the
restructuring of International Relations theory may be of discernible
actuality at the level of meta-theory, at the level of theoretical analysis
of concrete issues it remains little more than potentiality. Yet it is
clearly crucial to carry out this enterprise if the promise held out by
the meta-theoretical restructuring process identified in this study is to
be fulfilled.

Inevitably, a critical theory of international politics which is
committed to working for human emancipation will, virtually by
definition, come into conflict with 'certain vested interests – intellectual, political, economic, social in general'.[6] Even so, there is no
alternative. If International Relations theory is to remain 'true to its
moral commitment', the restructuring process now underway must be
brought to its 'subversive and revolutionary' conclusion.[7] It is only in
this way that the discipline of International Relations can hope to
make a meaningful contribution to the 'Aristotelian project' of the
'leading of a good and just life' in our global *polis*.

Notes

Introduction

1 'The Nature and Limits of a Theory of International Relations', in William T. R. Fox, ed., *Theoretical Aspects of International Relations* (Notre Dame, Ind.: University of Notre Dame Press, 1959), p. 16.

2 'Die gesellschaftliche Funktion der Philosophie', in Alfred Schmidt, ed., *Kritische Theorie: Eine Dokumentation* (Frankfurt: S. Fischer Verlag, 1968), II, p. 308, my translation.

3 Mark Hoffman, 'Critical Theory and the Inter-Paradigm Debate', *Millennium*, 16, No. 2 (1987), 231.

4 (New York: Harcourt Brace Jovanovich, 1976). Indeed, it was the title of Bernstein's work which provided the inspiration for that of the present study.

5 I say 'similar' rather than 'identical' for two reasons. First, rather than seeing 'critique' as one dimension of the restructuring process among others (along with, for example, an interpretive approach), in this study the notion of 'critical theory' is understood to subsume all of the elements of the restructuring process within it. (See chapter one below.)

Secondly, while I agree with Bernstein that the restructuring process must involve both a concern with achieving an interpretive understanding of the intersubjective meanings which constitute the social world, as well as an interest in criticizing that world as part of the effort to change it, I also argue that a third element of a critical restructuring is 'theoretical reflexivity': theoretical reflection upon the process of theorizing itself. (See chapter one below.) However, while 'theoretical reflexivity' was not featured in *The Restructuring of Social and Political Theory*, Bernstein does address this issue in his subsequent study, *Beyond Objectivism and Relativism* (Philadelphia: University of Pennsylvania Press, 1983) – a work upon which I draw heavily in my discussion of 'theoretical reflexivity'. (See chapter three below.)

6 I provide here a representative, though by no means exhaustive list of earlier work in this regard. See, for example, Richard K. Ashley, 'Political Realism and Human Interests', *International Studies Quarterly*, 25, No. 2 (1981), pp.

204–36, as well as Ashley, 'The Poverty of Neorealism', in R. O. Keohane, ed., *Neorealism and Its Critics* (New York: Columbia University Press, 1986); Robert W. Cox, 'Social Forces, States and World Orders: Beyond International Relations Theory', especially the 'Postscript 1985', also in Keohane, *Neorealism and Its Critics*; Mervyn Frost, *Towards a Normative Theory of International Relations* (Cambridge: Cambridge University Press, 1986); R. B. J. Walker, *Inside/Outside: International Relations as Political Theory* (Cambridge: Cambridge University Press, 1993); Andrew Linklater, *Beyond Realism and Marxism: Critical Theory and International Relations* (New York: St Martin's Press, 1990); as well as V. Spike Peterson, 'Introduction' to *Gendered States: Feminist (Re)Visions of International Relations Theory* (Boulder: Lynne Rienner, 1992); see also Richard Higgott, ed., *New Directions in International Relations? Australian Perspectives* (Canberra: The Australian National University, 1988), especially the contributions by Jim George ('International Relations and the Positivist Empiricist Theory of Knowledge') and David Campbell ('Recent Changes in Social Theory: Questions for International Relations'). More recent works in this vein are Claire Sjolander and Wayne Cox, eds., *Beyond Positivism: Critical Reflections on International Relations* (Boulder: Lynne Rienner, 1994) and Jim George, *Discourses of Global Politics* (Boulder: Lynne Rienner, 1994).

7 David Held, *Introduction to Critical Theory: Horkheimer to Habermas* (Berkeley: University of California Press, 1980), p. 184.

8 Held, *Introduction to Critical Theory*, p. 184. Indeed, given the traditional preoccupation with epistemology in the discipline of International Relations, it comes as little surprise that critiques constructed at the level of ontology have often met with just this charge.

9 Held, *Introduction to Critical Theory*, pp. 184–5.

10 See chapters three, four and five, below.

11 As was noted above, some of the current advocates of postmodernism in contemporary International Relations theorizing contributed, during the 1980s, trenchant critiques of positivism in the discipline. Some of those critiques, moreover, were constructed in terms very much in line with those of the Frankfurt School and, by extension, this study (Richard Ashley is the prime example – see note 6 above). For reasons discussed in later chapters, however, I do not follow these theorists beyond their critiques of positivism to adopt postmodernism as the optimal alternative to mainstream positivist theorizing.

1 International Relations theory and the Aristotelian project

1 'The Nature and Limits of a Theory of International Relations', in William T. R. Fox, ed., *Theoretical Aspects of International Relations* (Notre Dame, Ind.: University of Notre Dame Press, 1959), p. 16.

2 'Bemerkungen über Wissenschaft und Krise', in Alfred Schmidt, ed., *Kritische Theorie: Eine Dokumentation* (Frankfurt: S. Fischer Verlag, 1968), I, p. 7, my translation.

3 Richard J. Bernstein, *The Restructuring of Social and Political Theory* (New York: Harcourt Brace Jovanovich, 1976), p. xxii; Leonard Harris, 'Review of *The Restructuring of Social and Political Theory*', *International Philosophical Quarterly*, 19 (1979), p. 485.

4 Hannah Arendt, *The Human Condition* (Chicago: University of Chicago Press, 1958), pp. 13–14.

5 Thomas A. McCarthy, *The Critical Theory of Jürgen Habermas* (Cambridge, Mass.: MIT Press, 1978), p. 2.

6 Arendt, *The Human Condition*, p. 26.

7 Arendt, *The Human Condition*, p. 32.

8 *On Revolution* (New York: Viking Press, 1963), p. 23. See also Richard J. Bernstein, *Beyond Objectivism and Relativism* (Philadelphia: University of Pennsylvania Press, 1983), p. 208.

9 *The Human Condition*, p. 195.

10 *The Human Condition*, p. 198. Of course, it can be argued that in historical terms the 'golden age' of the Greek city-state deviated in many respects from the ideal contained in classical political theory: i.e. that those made 'free and equal' by the *polis* tended to be a narrow strata of men, with a sizeable female and slave underclass excluded from the noble interaction of unconstrained speech and action. Nonetheless, it is the regulative ideal of the *polis* as a 'realm of freedom' for all with which I am concerned here.

11 Charles Taylor, *Hegel and Modern Society* (Cambridge: Cambridge University Press, 1979), p. 93.

12 *Hegel and Modern Society*, p. 93. See also Andrew Linklater, *Men and Citizens in the Theory of International Relations* (London: Macmillan, 1982), pp. 146–9. As Linklater notes, Hegel opposed any doctrine of 'cosmopolitanism which took issue with the roles and responsibilities integral to the state' (p. 147). At the same time, however, Linklater also underscores the fact that there does appear to be a contradiction between Hegel's 'principle of human freedom, which demands the rational organization of political life, and the actual operations of the international states-system, the coercive or uncontrolled relations which pertain to the life of states' (p. 148). Avineri's argument that for Hegel, history involved the creation of a community of states within a world 'united by culture and reason' may be one way of resolving this contradiction. See Shlomo Avineri, *Hegel's Theory of the Modern State* (London: Cambridge University Press, 1972), p. 207. It may also serve to temper the Hegelian claim that 'the European state represented the highest form of political association' (Linklater, p. 149).

13 Linklater, *Men and Citizens*. It can be argued that Kant was preceded in theorizing the conceptual shift from the rights and freedoms of 'citizens' to 'persons' by Rousseau. See Linklater, *Men and Citizens*, *passim*. See also Michael C. Williams, 'Rousseau, Realism and Realpolitik', *Millennium*, 18, No. 2 (1989), pp. 188–204. It is also Linklater's contention that Kant's 'desire for a universal society of free individuals' stands at the centre of the theorizing of Karl Marx (p. 159).

14 The words are T. H. Green's from his *Prolegomena to Ethics* (Oxford, 1906), p. 283, and are quoted in Linklater, *Men and Citizens*, p. 208, note 20.

This is not to argue that Kant's understanding of 'politics' was in the tradition of classical political theory. On the differences, see Jürgen Habermas, 'The Classical Doctrine of Politics in Relation to Social Philosophy', in Habermas, *Theory and Practice*, trans. Jeremy J. Shapiro (Boston: Beacon Press, 1973), p. 42.

15 Including the nation-states system. See, for example, Richard Falk, *The End of World Order* (New York: Holmes & Meier, 1983). See also Linklater, *Men and Citizens*, p. 6. For a similar conclusion, this time from a realist perspective, see John Herz, *The Nation-State and the Crisis of World Politics* (New York: David McKay, 1976), pp. 15–19. Notes Herz, 'only a radical change in attitudes [in the direction of universalism] and policies could, in the long run, save the world from disaster', p. 15.

16 Falk, *The End of World Order*, p. 15.

It should be noted that Arendt herself, and despite her assertion that the *polis* could be created almost anywhere and any time, would most probably have had great difficulty in conceptualizing the *polis* in global terms. This is because Arendt held that only small groups of people allowed for the creative actions which distinguished the *polis*. In larger collectivities of people, argued Arendt, creative action was invariably supplanted by conformist behaviour. See Arendt, pp. 42–3. See also Terence Ball, 'Ontological Presuppositions and Political Consequences', in Daniel R. Sabia, Jr, and Jerald T. Wallulis, eds., *Changing Social Science* (Albany: State University of New York Press, 1983), pp. 40–2.

In response, one could argue that there is no reason why a world order created in conformity with the idea of the *polis* could not be based on loose federation of communities small enough to allow for the kind of creative, non-conformist behaviour Arendt fears is lost in larger groups. For an effort to theorize a global order in terms of the notion of a 'global *polis*' while attempting to accommodate the kind of concerns raised by Arendt, see Richard Falk, 'Anarchism and World Order', *Nomos*, 19 (1978).

17 Stanley Hoffmann, *Contemporary Theory in International Relations* (Englewood Cliffs, N.J.: Prentice-Hall, 1960), p. 4. Also quoted in Linklater, *Men and Citizens*, p. 5.

18 See Karl Deutsch, *The Analysis of International Relations*, 3rd edn (Englewood Cliffs, N.J.: Prentice-Hall, 1988), p. ix.

19 Robert O. Keohane, 'Theory of World Politics: Structural Realism and Beyond', in R. O. Keohane, ed., *Neorealism and Its Critics* (New York: Columbia University Press, 1986), p. 199. Keohane is clearly making reference to the work of Jonathan Schell. See J. Schell, *The Fate of the Earth* (New York: Alfred A. Knopf, 1982).

20 J. David Singer, 'The Responsibilities of Competence in the Global Village', *International Studies Quarterly*, 29, No. 3 (1985), p. 245.

21 'Realism, Marxism and Critical International Theory', *Review of International Studies*, 12, No. 4 (1986), p. 308. See also his *Beyond Realism and Marxism: Critical Theory and International Relations* (New York: St Martin's Press, 1990).

22 This historical review will focus on the Enlightenment origins of critical theory and, in particular, the evolution of the tradition through the eighteenth and nineteenth centuries. It is true, of course, that additional modifications and reformulations were made during the twentieth century, especially by those identified with the tradition of Western Marxism: Lukács, Korsch, Gramsci, and, of course, the members of the Frankfurt School, who adopted the term 'Critical Theory' to describe their work. Nonetheless, with Marx's contribution to the base already laid by Kant and Hegel, the broad outlines of critical theory which concern us here were already established.

23 Paul Connerton, editor's introduction to *Critical Sociology: Selected Readings* (New York: Penguin, 1976), p. 15. See also the heading 'critique' in the *Dictionary of Sociology* (2nd edn. London: Penguin, 1988), p. 56.

24 Of course, as Connerton notes, the weapon of critique was double-edged, as Catholics employed philological methods to demonstrate the very necessity of the Church tradition which Protestants were seeking to undermine. See Connerton, *Critical Sociology*, p. 15.

25 Connerton, *Critical Sociology*, p. 16.

26 *Ibid.*

27 See Jürgen Habermas, *Strukturwandel der Öffentlichkeit* (Berlin: Luchterhand, 1962).

28 Trans. Norman Kemp Smith (London: Macmillan, 1929), p. 9.

29 Literally, 'das Zeitalter der Kritik'.

30 'Beantwortung der Frage: Was ist Aufklärung?'. Quoted in Thomas A. McCarthy, *The Critical Theory of Jürgen Habermas* (Cambridge, Mass.: MIT Press, 1978), p. 77.

31 Connerton, *Critical Sociology*, p. 17.

32 Scott Warren, *The Emergence of Dialectical Theory: Philosophy and Political Inquiry* (Chicago: University of Chicago Press, 1984), p. 29.

33 *Ibid.*

34 That is, the exploration of the conditions through which modern natural science is possible. In part, Kant's relatively narrow conceptualization of epistemological issues can be traced to his assumption – not at all foreign to contemporary positivists – of a normative concept of science, with modern physics taken as the model of legitimate 'scientific knowledge'. See Jürgen Habermas, *Knowledge and Human Interests*, trans. Jeremy J. Shapiro (Boston: Beacon Press, 1971), pp. 13–15.

35 Linklater, *Men and Citizens*, p. 144.

36 It was the inability of Kant's epistemology to justify itself – to explain how the preconditions of knowledge are themselves already knowledge – that led Hegel to deem Kant's formulation a 'bad infinity' incapable of

serving as a 'first philosophy'. For a fuller discussion of this point, see Warren, *The Emergence of Dialectical Theory*, pp. 33–4.

37 It can be argued, as does Habermas, that in one sense, Hegel's reformulation did not so much radicalize epistemology as abolish it; that Hegel's 'philosophy of identity' subsumed epistemology within the notion of 'absolute knowledge' and thus left itself – and by extension, the entire tradition of critical theorizing – open to being discredited by the ensuing practical successes achieved by positivist natural sciences. See Habermas, *Knowledge and Human Interests*, chapter one. See also McCarthy, *The Critical Theory of Jürgen Habermas* Part I, as well as Garbis Kortian, *Métacritique* (Paris: Editions de Minuit, 1979), pp. 19–20.

38 John B. Thompson, *Critical Hermeneutics: A Study in the Thought of Paul Ricoeur and Jürgen Habermas* (Cambridge: Cambridge University Press, 1981), p. 72.

39 G. W. F. Hegel, *The Phenomenology of Mind*, trans. J. B. Baillie (New York: Harper & Row, 1967), pp. 81–2. Also quoted in Thompson, *Critical Hermeneutics*, p. 72.

40 Connerton, *Critical Sociology*, p. 19.

41 Warren, *The Emergence of Dialectical Theory*, p. 36, emphasis in the original.

42 Linklater, *Men and Citizens*, p. 146.

43 Connerton, *Critical Sociology*, p. 19.

44 Hegel himself provides an outstanding example of this kind of emancipation-oriented theoretical reflection which presents the idea of liberation from coercive illusions in his discussion of the Master–Slave relationship in the *Phenomenology of Mind*. The Master tries to make the Slave the instrument of his will. The Slave expresses himself in his productive activity and then recognizes that expression in the objects he has created. As a consequence, the Slave experiences himself as a subject. And it is in this way that the distorting pressures of slavery lead dialectically to the demand for freedom. For Hegel, the *Bildungsprozeß* evident in the Master–Slave relationship was a universal feature of human life and thought.

45 Warren, *The Emergence of Dialectical Theory*, p. 36.

46 Nor is it inappropriate to discuss Marx's theorizing in terms of the larger Aristotelian project. As the Western Marxist philosopher Georg Lukács noted, the entire Hegelian-inspired tradition of historicist Marxism can be understood as a form of left-wing Aristotelianism. See Tom Rockmore, ed., *Lukács Today: Essays in Marxist Philosophy* (Boston: D. Reidel Publishing Company, 1988), p. 5.

47 Linklater, *Men and Citizens*, p. 151.

48 See the discussion of Marx and 'critique' in the section dealing with the tradition of 'Western Marxism' in Tom Bottomore, ed., *Dictionary of Marxist Thought* (Cambridge, Mass.: Harvard University Press, 1983), pp. 523–6.

49 McCarthy, *The Critical Theory of Jürgen Habermas*, p. 55. McCarthy is para-

phrasing Habermas. See Habermas, *Knowledge and Human Interests*, p. 28.

50 'Der Achtzehnte Brumaire des Louis Bonaparte', in *Karl Marx und Friedrich Engels: Ausgewählte Werke* (Moscow: Progress Publishers, 1981), p. 99.

51 Steven Seidman, ed., Introduction to *Jürgen Habermas on Society and Politics: A Reader* (Boston: Beacon Press, 1989), p. 3.

52 Karl Marx, 'Introduction to the Critique of Hegel's Philosophy of Right', quoted in McCarthy, *The Critical Theory of Jürgen Habermas*, p. 16.

53 'Thesen über Feuerbach', in *Karl Marx und Friedrich Engels: Ausgewählte Werke*, p. 28.

54 'Conscientization' is the English transliteration of the Portuguese word *conscientizacção* by the Brazilian educator Paulo Freire. See P. Freire, *Pedagogy of the Oppressed* (New York: Continuum, 1983).

55 In addition to the influence of Bernstein noted in the Introduction, the three defining characteristics employed here were also inspired by and, at least in part, derived from those of 'reflexivity, the acceptance of a methodological and ontological orientation distinct from the naturalist paradigm, and a commitment to social criticism and advocacy' advanced by Sabia and Wallulis in their discussion of 'critical social science'. See Daniel R. Sabia, Jr, and Jerald T. Wallulis, 'The Idea of a Critical Social Science', in Sabia and Wallulis, *Changing Social Science*, pp. 6–7.

56 Karl Marx and Frederick Engels, *The German Ideology* (Moscow: Progress Publishers, 1968), p. 41; quoted in Nancy Fraser, 'What's Critical about Critical Theory?' in Seyla Benhabib and Drucilla Cornell, eds. *Feminism as Critique* (Minneapolis: University of Minnesota Press, 1986), p. 31.

2 Defining positivism

1 'The Nature and Limits of a Theory of International Relations', in William T. R. Fox, ed., *Theoretical Aspects of International Relations* (Notre Dame, Ind.: University of Notre Dame Press, 1959), pp. 19–20.

2 'Traditionelle und Kritische Theorie', in Alfred Schmidt, ed., *Kritische Theorie: Eine Dokumentation* (Frankfurt: S. Fischer Verlag, 1968), II, p. 137, my translation.

3 See Jürgen Habermas, 'The Classical Doctrine of Politics in Relation to Social Philosophy', in Habermas, *Theory and Practice* (Boston: Beacon Press, 1973), p. 44.

4 William Outhwaite, *New Philosophies of Social Science: Realism, Hermeneutics and Critical Theory* (Basingstoke: Macmillan, 1987), p. 5.

5 William Bechtel, *Philosophy of Science* (London: Lawrence Erlbaum, 1988), p. 18.

6 Outhwaite, *New Philosophies of Social Science*, p. 5.

7 *Ibid.*

8 For example, having counterposed the objective knowledge of positivism to the normatively distorted knowledge of theology and metaphysics, Comte began to reintroduce normative elements into positive knowledge

by speaking of the development of a positivist morality and politics. Similarly, Comte's teleological philosophy of human history was considered by later positivists to have disturbingly metaphysical overtones. See Outhwaite, *New Philosophies of Social Science*, pp. 5–6.

9 Bechtel, *Philosophy of Science*, p. 17. Another prominent philosopher of science associated with logical positivism – though in some ways more as a 'friendly critic' than a core adherent – was Karl Popper.

10 Symbolic logic, to be distinguished from Aristotelian 'syllogistic logic', is composed of 'sentential' or 'propositional' logic on the one hand and 'quantificational logic' (also known as 'predicate calculus') on the other. For an extended discussion of the development and characteristics of symbolic logic, see Bechtel, *Philosophy of Science*, pp. 3–8.

11 See above, note 8.

12 This discussion is based heavily on Bechtel, *Philosophy of Science*, pp. 19–31, and Fred R. Dallmayr, *Language and Politics* (Notre Dame, Ind.: University of Notre Dame Press, 1984), pp. 28–52. For parallel discussions, see Fred R. Dallmayr and Thomas A. McCarthy, *Understanding and Social Inquiry* (Notre Dame, Ind.: University of Notre Dame Press, 1977), pp. 77–9, as well as Brian Fay, *Social Theory and Political Practice* (London: George Allen & Unwin, 1975), chapter two.

13 See Dallmayr, *Language and Politics*, p. 29.

14 Bechtel, *Philosophy of Science*, p. 19.

15 Bechtel, *Philosophy of Science*, p. 20.

16 *Ibid.*

17 Dallmayr, *Language and Politics*, p. 30. As Dallmayr notes, one of the most committed defenders of the referential theory of meaning was the philosopher Bertrand Russell. See Dallmayr, pp. 29–32.

18 Dallmayr, *Language and Politics*, p. 36.

19 Bechtel, *Philosophy of Science*, p. 20.

20 Dallmayr, *Language and Politics*, pp. 36–7. An important exception, of course, are strictly syntactical–analytical propositions.

21 Schlick, quoted in Dallmayr, *Language and Politics*, pp. 37–8.

22 Bechtel, *Philosophy of Science*, p. 20. An example is the statement 'The sky is blue.'

One of the most staunchly argued positions was that of 'physicalism' – the position that 'basic report sentences can and should be stated in physicalist language, that is, in the form of quantitative descriptions referring to concrete space-time points'. A position championed by both Neurath and Carnap, the chief advantage to descriptions formulated in physicalist terms is held to be their 'reliance on (presumably) inter-sensual or intersubjective data'. See Dallmayr, *Language and Politics*, p. 34.

23 Karl-Otto Apel, *Die Idee der Sprache in der Tradition des Humanismus von Dante bis Vico*, 3rd edn (Bonn: Bouvier, 1980), p. 29, quoted in Dallmayr, *Language and Politics*, p. 29.

24 Bechtel, *Philosophy of Science*, p. 20.

A derivation of symbolic logic holding particular importance for the research design of logical positivism is the *modus ponens* or 'affirming the antecedent' (A is the analytical statement; B is the synthetic statement) :

If A, then B.

A_____

Therefore, B.

As Bechtel notes (p. 21), this effort to
> explicate the meaning of all scientific discourse in terms of observation conditions is closely related to the very influential doctrine, associated with the American physicist and mathematician Percy Bridgman, of operational definitions. According to this doctrine, in introducing a theoretical concept, it is necessary to specify operations through which one can confirm or disconfirm statements using that term. Bridgman's notion of an operational definition extends the Positivists' conception of an observation term by supplying procedures for producing the requisite observations.'

25 Bechtel, *Philosophy of Science*, pp. 21–2.
26 Schlick, quoted in Dallmayr, *Language and Politics*, p. 38. Typical is Carnap's response to Heidegger's essay 'What is Metaphysics?':
> in the domain of metaphysics, including all philosophy of value and normative theory, logical analysis yields the negative result that the alleged statements in this domain are entirely meaningless.
> Quoted in Dallmayr, *Language and Politics*, p. 36.

27 Bechtel, *Philosophy of Science*, p. 19.
28 Bechtel, *Philosophy of Science*, p. 22.
29 *Ibid*.
30 Karl Popper, *The Logic of Scientific Discovery* (London: Hutchinson, 1968), pp. 59–60.
31 Bechtel, *Philosophy of Science*, p. 23.
32 Fay, *Social Theory and Political Practice*, pp. 32–3.
33 Fay, *Social Theory and Political Practice*, p. 33.
34 Fay, *Social Theory and Political Practice*, p. 37. Hempel was particularly concerned to modify the deductive–nomological/covering law form of explanation to allow for 'inductive–statistical' explanations. See Bechtel, *Philosophy of Science*, p. 24.
35 Bechtel, *Philosophy of Science*, p. 24.
36 For further discussion of the distinction between the 'context of discovery' and the 'context of justification', see Frederich Suppe, *The Structure of Scientific Theories*, 2nd edn (Urbana: University of Illinois Press, 1977), p. 125.
37 Note that it is of no consequence how we have arrived at this hypothesis – a question relating to the 'context of discovery'.
38 Of course, should we ever notice, all things being equal, that water does *not* boil at 100°C, we can consider the general proposition relating the

boiling of water to its temperature disconfirmed, thereby ensuring that the quest to specify the causal relationship between temperature and boiling (if any) will be reopened.

39 Fay, *Social Theory and Political Practice*, p. 31.
40 Bechtel, *Philosophy of Science*, p. 25, emphasis in the original.
41 Bechtel, *Philosophy of Science*, p. 28.
42 *Ibid.*
43 *Ibid.*
44 One of the more important modifications was the shift in emphasis, stemming from the work of Karl Popper, from confirmation of true hypotheses to the falsification of untrue hypotheses.
45 Bechtel, *Philosophy of Science*, p. 29.
46 For Popper's and Lakatos' contribution of the notions of (methodological) 'falsification' and 'sophisticated methodological falsificationism', respectively, see Popper, *The Logic of Scientific Discovery* and Imre Lakatos, 'Falsification and the Methodology of Scientific Research Programmes', in I. Lakatos and A. Musgrave, eds., *Criticism and the Growth of Knowledge* (London: Cambridge University Press, 1970). For a good introduction to the contributions of Popper and Lakatos, see A. F. Chalmers, *What is This Thing Called Science?, 2nd edn (St Lucia, Queensland: University of Queensland Press, 1982).*
47 For another effort to identify the distinguishing characteristics of the positivist tradition as a whole – one which does so in terms of four 'rules' – see Leszek Kolakowski, *The Alienation of Reason: A History of Positivist Thought*, trans. Norbert Guterman (New York: Doubleday, 1968).
48 For a discussion of the on-going movement of fallibilistic positivist science toward an ever closer approximation to the truth (understood as correspondence to objective reality) – in Popper's terms, 'verisimilitude' – see Karl Popper, *Conjectures and Refutations: The Growth of Scientific Knowledge*, 3rd edn (London: Routledge and Kegan Paul, 1969), chapter 10.
49 It should be noted that 'facts' have a special status in positivism: 'Facts' refer 'to a class of phenomena which were believed to be in some manner ... "given" in immediate experience and represented in an indefeasible observation language.' Gunnell, 'Philosophy and Political Theory', *Government and Opposition*, 14, No. 2, p. 208. Quoted in Roger Tooze, 'International Political Economy', in Steve Smith, ed., *International Relations: British and American Perspectives* (Oxford: Blackwell, 1985), p. 113.
50 Arnold Brecht, *Political Theory: The Foundations of Twentieth-Century Political Thought* (Princeton, N.J.: Princeton University Press, 1959), p. 481, quoted in Scott Warren, *The Emergence of Dialectical Theory: Philosophy and Political Inquiry* (Chicago: University of Chicago Press, 1984), p. 8.
51 *The Theory and Method of Political Analysis* (Homewood, Ill.: Dorsey Press, 1965), p. 12, quoted in Warren, *The Emergence of Dialectical Theory*, p. 8.

52 *The Political System: An Inquiry into the State of Political Science* (New York: Alfred A. Knopf, 1953), pp. 225–6, quoted in Warren, *The Emergence of Dialectical Theory*, p. 11.

53 *Modern Political Analysis* (Englewood Cliffs, N.J.: Prentice-Hall, 1963), p. 8.

54 George E. G. Catlin, *A Study of the Principles of Politics* (London: Allen & Unwin, 1930), p. 39.

55 *The Political System*, pp. 78, 86, 89, quoted in Warren, *The Emergence of Dialectical Theory*, p. 9.

56 *The Poverty of Historicism* (New York: Harper and Row, 1961), pp. 1–2, quoted in Fred Gareau, 'The Long, Uncertain Road to Social Science Maturity', *International Journal of Cognitive Sociology*, 29, No. 3–4, (1988), p. 178.

57 Easton, *The Political System*, pp. 3–4, quoted in Warren, *The Emergence of Dialectical Theory*, p. 7.

58 Nor has the adoption of the scientific method, to the degree that it has occurred, been uniform across the social sciences. Notes Easton:

> If the condition of political science represented the exhaustion of its present potentialities, then there would be little justification in voicing any concern about it. But comparison with the level of achievement of other social sciences demonstrates what political science could be doing. However much students of political life may seek to escape the taint, if they were to eavesdrop on the whisperings of their fellow social scientists, they would find that they are almost generally stigmatized as the least advanced. They could present society, they would hear, with at least a slice of bread but they offer it only a crumb.
>
> *The Political System*, p. 40, quoted in Warren,
> *The Emergence of Dialectical Theory*, p. 7.

59 Kaspar D. Naegele, 'Some Observations on the Scope of Sociological Analysis', in T. Parsons, M. Shils, and E. Naegele, eds., *Theories of Society: Foundations of Modern Sociological Theory* (New York: The Free Press, 1961), I, p. 3.

60 Eugene J. Meehan, *Value Judgement and Social Science: Structures and Processes* (Homewood, Ill.: Dorsey Press, 1969), p. 147, quoted in Warren, *The Emergence of Dialectical Theory*, p. 9.

61 Easton, *The Political System*, p. 45, quoted in Warren, *The Emergence of Dialectical Theory*, p. 9.

62 *The Political System*, p. 225, quoted in Warren, *The Emergence of Dialectical Theory*, p. 11, my emphasis.

63 Easton quoted in Warren, *The Emergence of Dialectical Theory*, p. 10.

64 Easton, *The Political System*, p. 221, quoted in Warren, *The Emergence of Dialectical Theory*, p. 10, my emphasis.

65 Alan Isaak, *Scope and Methods of Political Science: An Introduction to the Methodology of Political Inquiry* (Homewood, Ill.: Dorsey Press, 1969), p. 56, quoted in Warren, *The Emergence of Dialectical Theory*, p. 11.

66 Popper, for example, felt that the logical positivists went too far in asserting that value questions were 'meaningless'.

67 On this point, see Dante Germino, *Beyond Ideology: The Revival of Political Theory* (New York: Harper and Row, 1967), p. 83.
68 Heinz Eulau, *The Behavioural Persuasion in Politics* (New York: Random House, 1964), p. 133, quoted in Warren, *The Emergence of Dialectical Theory*, p. 10.

3 Reflexivity and International Relations theory

1 'The Nature and Limits of a Theory of International Relations', in William T. R. Fox, ed., *Theoretical Aspects of International Relations* (Notre Dame, Ind.: University of Notre Dame Press, 1959), p. 21.
2 *Knowledge and Human Interests*, trans. Jeremy J. Shapiro (Boston: Beacon Press, 1971), p. vii, emphasis in the original.
3 Yosef Lapid, 'The Third Debate: On the Prospects of International Theory in a Post-Positivist Era', *International Studies Quarterly*, 33, No. 3 (1989), pp. 249–50.
4 Although conceived independently, the elements of the definition of reflexivity being advanced here are closely paralleled by those proposed by Connolly under the rubric of 'theoretical self-consciousness', defined as

> first, an effort to clarify for self and others the basic presumptions and conceptual organization of the perspective brought to inquiry; second, an assessment of the extent to which the available evidence supports or contravenes the perspective; third, a full statement of the normative import of the theory; and finally, an assessment of the extent to which available evidence and other explicit considerations justify acting in support of those normative conclusions.

> See William Connolly, 'Theoretical Self-Consciousness', in William Connolly and Glen Gordon, eds., *Social Structure and Political Theory* (London: D. C. Heath, 1974), pp. 57–8.

5 And so it remains. Imre Lakatos' neo-positivist 'methodology of scientific research programmes' is the most recent reformulation of the positivist tradition, and because of its current popularity among International Relations theorists, it bears special mention. The central distinctions between Lakatos' formulation and that of his teacher, Karl Popper, are (i) Lakatos' rejection of Popper's 'strict falsificationism', (ii) his shift of emphasis from individual statements to meta-theoretical units, i.e. 're-search programmes', as the proper concern of the philosophy of science (a shift which is thoroughly consistent with trends in social and political theory more generally), and (iii) his advocacy of tolerance of theoretical pluralism. Nonetheless, Lakatos' 'sophisticated methodological falsifica-tionism', like Popper's 'methodological falsificationism' before it, con-tinues to uphold the core tenets of the positivist logic of investigation: namely, (i) value-freedom in scientific knowledge, (ii) the methodological unity of science, and, most importantly in terms of the concerns of this chapter, (iii) the correspondence theory of truth.

On the latter point, note Lakatos' affirmation that 'the methodology of scientific research programmes is better suited for *approximating the truth in our actual universe* than any other methodology'. Quoted in A. F. Chalmers, *What is This Thing Called Science?*, 2nd edn (St Lucia, Queensland: University of Queensland Press, 1982), p. 104, emphasis added. Accordingly, it would seem that if Keohane's modernist–positivist reading of Lakatos' philosophy of science is untenable, his reading is nonetheless consistent with Lakatos' own understanding of what ends his work is intended to serve. See Robert O. Keohane, 'International Institutions: Two Approaches', *International Studies Quarterly*, 32, No. 4 (1988), pp. 379–96, and Richard K. Ashley and R. B. J. Walker, 'Speaking the Language of Exile', *International Studies Quarterly*, 34, No. 3 (1990), pp. 259–68.

6 It is true, of course, that neo-positivists such as Karl Popper implicitly acknowledged the theory-dependent nature of empirical evidence, a recognition which would seem to pose considerable problems for the notion of truth as correspondence. Despite this recognition, however, 'truth as correspondence' remained the regulative ideal of positivist social science, while the difficulties posed by theory-dependence were addressed in the efforts to specify 'rules of correspondence'.

7 The expression is Richard Rorty's. See his *Consequences of Pragmatism* (Brighton: Harvester, 1982), p. xxvi.

8 For a useful introduction to these traditions, see Jim George and David Campbell, 'Patterns of Dissent and the Celebration of Difference: Critical Social Theory and International Relations', *International Studies Quarterly*, 34, no. 3 (1990), pp. 269–94.

9 Cornel West, *The American Evasion of Philosophy* (Madison: The University of Wisconsin Press, 1989), p. 201, my emphasis.

10 West, *The American Evasion of Philosophy*, p. 201.

11 It is important not to confuse the notion of the inherently politico-normative content of paradigms with the considerably less radical argument (in that it remained consistent with the regulative ideal of 'truth as correspondence') advanced by post-behaviouralists: i.e., that scholars needed to become more aware of their personal 'value biases' and the way these could 'distort' the accuracy of empirical findings. In contrast, the argument from theoretical reflexivity is (i) that the (politico-) normative dimension of scholarship is not the property of individual scholars but adheres to the process of scholarly inquiry itself; (ii) that the politico-normative content of scholarship is not a 'contamination' of empirical research, but, in fact, constitutive of all such research (e.g., in determining what will count as a fact). For a clear statement of the post-behavioural position on values and social science, see David Easton, 'The New Revolution in Political Science', in Easton, *The Political System: An Inquiry Into the State of Political Science*, 2nd edn (New York: Alfred A. Knopf, 1971), pp. 323–48.

12 See chapter five below.

13 For a useful discussion of the distinction between natural and social

sciences in terms of the incommensurability thesis, see Steven Lukes, *Moral Conflict and Politics* (Oxford: Clarendon Press, 1991), chapter three.

14 Karl Popper, 'Normal Science and Its Dangers', in I. Lakatos and A. Musgrave, eds., *Criticism and the Growth of Knowledge* (London: Cambridge University Press, 1970), p. 56.

15 The fact that a neutral observation language cannot be used to adjudicate normative claims is, of course, recognized by positivists as well, and goes a long way in explaining traditional positivist antipathy to debates about the validity of competing normative claims.

It is also important that the difference between paradigms not be seen as one of a simple conflict over values – a position which implies that while agreement on the facts is possible, disagreement over values lies at the root of the failure to achieve intersubjective consensus. Values may indeed differ across paradigms, but the notion of what is to count as a fact is equally contested.

16 As Bernstein notes in his review of the 'father of modern philosophy':

> With a chilling clarity Descartes leads us with an apparent and ineluctable necessity to a grand and seductive Either/Or. *Either* there is some support for our being, a fixed foundation for our knowledge, *or* we cannot escape the forces of darkness that envelop us with madness, with intellectual and moral chaos.
>
> See Richard J. Bernstein, *Beyond Objectivism and Relativism: Science, Hermeneutics, and Praxis* (Philadelphia: University of Pennsylvania Press, 1983), p. 18, emphasis in the original.

17 Charles Taylor, 'The Diversity of Goods' in his *Philosophy and the Human Sciences* (Cambridge: Cambridge University Press, 1985), p. 230.

It is, of course, true that only the logical positivists advocated the extreme position that normative claims were just so much 'nonsense', and that others in the positivist tradition – Popper, for example – were more sympathetic to the idea that normative theorizing could produce knowledge. So strong is the notion of 'truth as correspondence' in the positivist tradition, however, that even the most sympathetic have been hard pressed to explain how reason could serve in assessing the truth value of normative claims.

18 Charles Taylor, *Hegel and Modern Society* (Cambridge: Cambridge University Press, 1979), p. 64.

19 Hans-Georg Gadamer, *Truth and Method* (New York: Crossroad, 1988).

20 Jürgen Habermas, *The Theory of Communicative Action*, trans. Thomas McCarthy (Boston: Beacon Press, 1984).

21 *Beyond Objectivism and Relativism.* According to Bernstein (p. 86, emphasis in the original),

> Kuhn did not introduce the incommensurability thesis in order to call into the question the possibility of *comparing* theories and rationally evaluating them, but to clarify what we are *doing* when we compare [incommensurable] theories.

22 An example of how a judgment about contending paradigms may be made on the basis of their politico-normative content is provided by Connolly. He argues that where evidence is insufficient to dictate the choice between competing theories in social science (as is the case when incommensurability obtains), a certain presumption should operate in favour of the theory which is more optimistic. His reasoning is as follows:

> concepts and beliefs about social life help to some degree to constitute that life. Therefore, privileging the more optimistic assumption ... might well help both to bring out evidence in its support previously unavailable *and to contribute itself* to the optimistic possibility. Thus the shared belief in a society that people *must* seek aggressively to exploit others justifies that conduct on the part of the privileged and contributes thereby to the assurance that such relationships are inevitable. Similarly, conduct based on more optimistic beliefs can sometimes contribute to their fulfilment.

'Theoretical Self-Consciousness', p. 64, emphasis in the original. Of course, one might well dispute Connolly's reasoning in developing his guidelines for theory choice. Still, aside from the specifics of his position, what is worth noting is that he is engaging in a form of reasoned assessment of incommensurable frameworks in terms of their politico-normative content.

23 Lapid, 'The Third Debate', p. 236.

24 See E. H. Carr, *The Twenty-Years' Crisis, 1919–1939: An Introduction to the Study of International Relations* (London: Macmillan, 1939).

25 For a collection of contributions to this second debate, see Klaus Knorr and James N. Rosenau, eds., *Contending Approaches to International Politics* (Princeton, N.J.: Princeton University Press, 1969).

26 Mark Hoffman, 'Critical Theory and the Inter-Paradigm Debate', *Millennium*, 16, No. 2 (1987), p. 231.

27 Michael Banks, 'The Inter-Paradigm Debate', in Margot Light and A. J. R. Groom, eds., *International Relations: A Handbook of Current Theory* (London: Pinter, 1985), p. 20.

28 Lapid, 'The Third Debate', p. 239.

29 Banks, 'The Inter-Paradigm Debate', p. 9.

30 'The Inter-Paradigm Debate', p. 12.

31 'The Inter-Paradigm Debate', pp. 12–13.

32 'The Inter-Paradigm Debate', p. 13.

33 *Ibid.*

34 Apart from disagreeing on the content and labels of contending paradigms, authors also disagree on the issue of the number of relevant paradigms, some identifying many more than three. Three does seem to be the most common number, however, and in this regard Banks is once again representative.

35 *The Dividing Discipline: Hegemony and Diversity in International Theory* (Boston: Allen & Unwin, 1985).

36 *International Relations Theory: Realism, Pluralism, Globalism* (New York: Macmillan, 1987).
37 *Global Problems and World Order* (Madison: University of Wisconsin Press, 1986).

Similarly, in his overview of the sub-field of international political economy, Robert Gilpin speaks in terms of the 'Nationalist', 'Liberal', and 'Marxist' perspectives. See his *The Political Economy of International Relations* (Princeton, N.J.: Princeton University Press, 1987).
38 Michael Banks, as quoted in Lapid, 'The Third Debate', p. 235.
39 Lapid, 'The Third Debate', p. 237.
40 See Lapid, 'The Third Debate', pp. 249–50.
41 As has already been noted, my notion of 'theoretical reflexivity', and of the three possible stances, is inspired by and derivative of Richard Bernstein's *Beyond Objectivism and Relativism*. See especially Part Two.
42 For Holsti's interventions, see *The Dividing Discipline*, as well as his response to Lapid, 'Mirror, Mirror on the Wall, Which are the Fairest Theories of All?', *International Studies Quarterly*, 33, No. 3, (1989), 255–61.
43 'Mirror, Mirror', pp. 255–6, my emphasis.
44 'Mirror, Mirror', p. 256.
45 'Mirror, Mirror', p. 259.
46 'Mirror, Mirror', p. 256.
47 *Ibid.*
48 *Ibid.*
49 *The Dividing Discipline*, p. viii.
50 'Mirror, Mirror', p. 258, emphasis in the original.
51 *The Dividing Discipline*, p. vii.
52 'Mirror, Mirror', p. 257.
53 'Mirror, Mirror', p. 259.
54 'Mirror, Mirror', p. 255.
55 'Commensurable and therefore comparable'.
56 Indeed, as McKinlay and Little observe, with obvious reference to those who have adopted 'Stance I', it is the refusal of those engaged in the Third Debate to acknowledge the ideological character of their work that leads them into 'endowing their model with a spurious empirical or scientific validity, which is made all the more striking in contrast to the mere "ideology" offered by other models'. *Global Problems and World Order*, p. 272.
57 Steve Smith, 'Paradigm Dominance in International Relations: The Development of International Relations as a Social Science', *Millennium*, 16, No. 2 (1987), pp. 189–206.
58 The employment of the word 'guide' is meant to indicate realism's importance for the practice of state managers in both a 'practical' as well as a 'technical/instrumental' sense. For a discussion of the distinction between the two senses as manifest in the realist tradition, see Richard K.

Ashley, 'Political Realism and Human Interests', *International Studies Quarterly*, 25, No. 2 (1981), pp. 204–36.
59 Smith, 'Paradigm Dominance', p. 197.
60 'Paradigm Dominance', p. 202. 'After all', notes Smith, 'if you are not a great power, in Morgenthau's use of the term, what foreign policy options do you have?' (p. 201).
61 Hayward R. Alker, Jr and Thomas J. Biersteker, 'The Dialectics of World Order: Notes for a Future Archaeologist of International Savoir Faire', *International Studies Quarterly*, 28, No. 2 (1984), pp. 138–9.
62 'The Dialectics of World Order', p. 139. For Alker and Biersteker's efforts to link contending paradigms to particular political agendas, see Figure 4, p. 138.
63 'The Dialectics of World Order', p. 267.
64 *Ibid.*
65 'The Dialectics of World Order', pp. 269, 270.
66 'The Dialectics of World Order', pp. 272–3.
67 Theodor Adorno, *Negative Dialectics*, trans. E. B. Ashton (New York: Continuum, 1973), p. 197.
68 See James N. Rosenau, 'Order and Disorder in the Study of World Politics', in R. Marghoori and B. Ramberg, eds., *Globalism Versus Realism: International Relations Third Debate* (Boulder: Westview, 1982), pp. 4, 5.

Rosenau also affirms that 'temperaments tend to remain ... fixed and resistant to new evidence' (p. 7), underscoring further the impotence and irrelevance of reasoned argumentation in the process of paradigm choice.
69 Another intervention which would fit into this category is that of Richard W. Mansbach and Yale H. Ferguson, *The Elusive Quest: Theory and International Politics* (Columbia, S.C.: University of South Carolina Press, 1988). In addition, certain of Gilpin's comments in his *The Political Economy of International Relations* might also qualify him as at least a part-time proponent of the stance of 'incommensurable and therefore incomparable'.
70 McKinlay and Little, *Global Problems and World Order*, p. 273.
71 Robert W. Cox, 'Social Forces, States and World Orders: Beyond International Relations Theory', in Robert O. Keohane, ed., *Neorealism and Its Critics* (New York: Columbia University Press, 1986), pp. 207, 217, emphasis in the original. Cox's piece was first published in 1981 in *Millennium*, 10, No. 2 (1982), pp. 126–55. Cox (p. 207) notes further that:
> All theories have a perspective. Perspectives derive from a position in time and space, specifically social and political time and space. The world is seen from a standpoint definable in terms of nation or social class, of dominance or subordination, of rising or declining power, of a sense of immobility or of present crisis, of past experience, and of hopes and expectations for the future.
72 Cox, 'Social Forces, States and World Orders', p. 207.
73 'Social Forces, States and World Orders', pp. 207–8.
74 *Ibid.*, my emphasis.

75 'Social Forces, States and World Orders', p. 208.
76 *Ibid.*
77 *Ibid.*
78 'Social Forces, States and World Orders', p. 209.
79 *Ibid.*
80 'Social Forces, States and World Orders', p. 210.
81 That is, its ability to produce cumulative, law-based explanations of 'reality' which can serve as guides to action.
82 See Stephen Gill, ed., *Gramsci, Historical Materialism and International Relations* (Cambridge: Cambridge University Press, 1993), especially the introduction.
83 Jim George, *Discourses of Global Politics: A Critical (Re)Introduction to International Relations* (Boulder: Lynne Rienner, 1994), p. 30, emphasis in the original.
84 *Discourses of Global Politics*, p. 191, emphasis in the original.
85 Foucault's exploration of power–knowledge discourses, already noted, stands as the clearest example.
86 Richard K. Ashley, 'The Geopolitics of Geopolitical Space: Toward a Critical Social Theory of International Politics', *Alternatives*, 12, No. 4 (1987), p. 408.
87 For an accessible overview of postmodernist contributions to the study of world politics, and to which this discussion is deeply indebted, see George, *Discourses of Global Politics*, especially chapter eight.
88 See R. B. J. Walker, 'The Prince and the "Pauper": Tradition, Modernity and Practice in the Theory of International Relations', in James Der Derian and Michael J. Shapiro, eds., *International/Intertextual Relations: Postmodern Readings of World Politics* (Toronto: Lexington Books, 1989).
89 See James Der Derian, *On Diplomacy: A Genealogy of Western Estrangement* (Oxford: Basil Blackwell, 1987).
90 See Bradley Klein, *Strategic Studies and World Order* (Cambridge: Cambridge University Press, 1994).
91 See, for example, Martin Jay's discussion of Foucault, in *Marxism and Totality* (Los Angeles: University of California Press, 1984), 'Epilogue', pp. 510–37.
92 Richard J. Bernstein, *The New Constellation: The Ethical–Political Horizons of Modernity/Postmodernity* (Oxford: Polity Press, 1991), p. 151, emphasis in the original. The argument that postmodernism suffers from a 'performative contradiction' has been put most forcefully by Habermas. See, for example, *The Philosophical Discourse of Modernity: Twelve Lectures* (Cambridge: Policy Press, 1987).
93 Quoted in Jay, *Marxism and Totality*, p. 526, emphasis in the original.
94 Jay, *Marxism and Totality*, p. 526.
95 See, for example, Pauline Rosenau, 'Once Again Into the Fray: International Relations Confronts the Humanities', *Millennium*, 19, No. 1 (1990), pp. 83–110.

96 Jim George and David Campbell, 'Patterns of Dissent and the Celebration of Difference: Critical Social Theory and International Relations', *International Studies Quarterly*, 34, No. 3 (1990), p. 289.
97 Richard K. Ashley and R. B. J. Walker, 'Reading Dissidence/Writing the Discipline: Crisis and the Question of Sovereignty in International Studies', *International Studies Quarterly*, 34, No. 3 (1990), p. 389.
98 'Reading Dissidence', p. 389.
99 Ashley, 'Living on the Border Lines: Man, Poststructuralism, and War', in Der Derian and Shapiro, *International/Intertextual Relations*, p. 278, my emphasis.
100 See Mark Hoffman, 'Critical Theory and the Inter-Paradigm Debate', *Millennium*, 16, No. 2 (1987), pp. 231–49; N. J. Rengger, 'Going Critical? A Response to Hoffman', *Millennium*, 17, No. 1 (1988), pp. 81–9; Mark Hoffman, 'Conversations on Critical International Relations Theory', *Millennium*, 17, No. 1, pp. 91–5.
101 'Going Critical?', p. 83.
102 *Ibid.*
103 'Going Critical?', p. 85. The phrase is Thomas Nagel's.
104 For example, Cox's rejection of problem-solving theory on the grounds that it 'rests upon a false premise, since the social and political order is not fixed but ... is changing' ('Social Forces, States and World Orders', p. 209) is a clear foundationalist appeal to the 'true nature' of reality – an appeal which is arguably in contradiction to a reflexive stance.
105 This epistemological category, like those which follow it ('feminist standpoint' and 'feminist postmodernism') are, of course, taken from the well-known work of Sandra Harding. See her *The Science Question in Feminism* (Ithaca, N.Y.: Cornell University Press, 1986).
106 Mary Hawkesworth, quoted in Anne Sisson Runyan and V. Spike Peterson, 'The Radical Future of Realism: Feminist Subversions of IR Theory', *Alternatives*, 16, No. 1 (1991), p. 72. Examples of feminist empiricism in the study of world politics are: Betsy Thom, 'Women in International Organizations: Room at the Top: The Situation in Some United Nations Organizations', in C. F. Epstein and R. L. Coser, eds., *Access to Power: Cross-National Studies of Women and Elites* (London: George Allen & Unwin, 1981), and Carol Riegelman Lubin and Anne Winslow, *Social Justice for Women: The International Labour Organizations and Women* (Durham: Duke University Press, 1990).
107 V. Spike Peterson, 'Introduction' to *Gendered States: Feminist (Re)Visions of International Relations Theory* (Boulder: Lynne Rienner, 1992), p. 19, emphasis in the original.
108 Peterson, *Gendered States*, p. 18, emphasis in the original.
109 Sarah Brown, 'Feminism, International Theory, and International Relations of Gender Inequality', *Millennium*, 17, No. 3 (1988), p. 472.
110 Hawkesworth, quoted in Runyan and Peterson, 'The Radical Future of Realism', pp. 73–4.

111 Runyan and Peterson, 'The Radical Future of Realism', p. 74.
112 *Ibid.*, emphasis in the original.
113 Hawkesworth, quoted in Runyan and Peterson, 'The Radical Future of Realism', pp. 74–5.
114 Marysia Zalewski, 'Feminist Theory and International Relations', in Mike Bowker and Robin Brown, eds., *From Cold War to Collapse: Theory and World Politics in the 1980s* (Cambridge: Cambridge University Press, 1993), pp. 136–7.
   Postmodernism's problematic treatment of the subject will be taken up in chapter five below.
115 Sandra Whitworth, 'Gender in the Inter-Paradigm Debate', *Millennium*, 18, No. 2 (1989), pp. 265–72.
116 Zalewski, 'Feminist Theory and International Relations', p. 140.
117 *Feminist Theory and International Relations in a Postmodern Era* (Cambridge: Cambridge University Press, 1994).
118 *Feminist Theory and International Relations in a Postmodern Era*, p. 63.
119 *Feminist Theory and International Relations in a Postmodern Era*, p. 14.
120 Kathy Ferguson, quoted in Sylvester, *Feminist Theory and International Relations in a Postmodern Era*, p. 63.
121 Whitworth, Review of Christine Sylvester, *Feminist Theory and International Relations in a Postmodern Era*, in *Canadian Journal of Political Science*, 28, No. 1 (1995), p. 178. In Whitworth's words, when Sylvester 'suggests that socialist feminism is the appropriate politics of postmodern feminism, she is trying to pull an el(l)e-phant out of a hat'.
122 Smith, 'Paradigm Dominance', p. 202, my emphasis.
123 The original reads 'The sort of philosophy one chooses thus depends on what sort of person one is.' Quoted in J. Habermas, *Knowledge and Human Interests*, p. 208.

4 Human consciousness and International Relations theory

1 'The Nature and Limits of a Theory of International Relations', in William T. R. Fox, ed., *Theoretical Aspects of International Relations* (Notre Dame, Ind.: University of Notre Dame Press, 1959), p. 21.
2 *The New Science of Giambattista Vico* (1744), trans. Thomas Goddard Bergin and Max Harold Fisch (Ithaca, N.Y.: Cornell University Press, 1984), para. 331, p. 96.
3 Also sometimes referred to as 'hermeneutics'.
4 On this point, see Fred R. Dallmayr and Thomas A. McCarthy, eds., *Understanding and Social Inquiry* (Notre Dame, Ind.: University of Notre Dame Press, 1977), pp. 77–80. The positivist philosopher Otto Neurath has equated *Verstehen* techniques with a 'cup of coffee': something which might increase the 'serendipity' of the social scientist, but which has no place in empirical work. See Dallmayr and McCarthy, *Understanding and Social Inquiry*, p. 6.

5 For example, in designing questionnaires, guiding the researcher in the interview process, etc.

6 Thomas A. McCarthy, *The Critical Theory of Jürgen Habermas*, (Cambridge, Mass.: MIT Press, 1978), p. 153.

7 It can, of course, be argued that 'meaning-oriented behaviouralists' have brought 'subjective meanings' into the public realm only by operationalizing those meanings in terms of specific forms of behaviour – i.e., a specific opinion on an issue is operationalized in terms of a specific response to a question in an opinion survey. From this perspective, what is being correlated is not a 'subjective meaning' with a specific behaviour, but rather one type of behaviour (e.g., the response to an opinion survey) with another (e.g., a vote in an election).

8 Paul Rabinow and William M. Sullivan, 'The Interpretive Turn', in P. Rabinow and W. Sullivan, eds., *Interpretive Social Science: A Second Look*, rev. edn (Berkeley: University of California Press, 1987), p. 7.

9 Charles Taylor, 'Interpretation and the Sciences of Man', in Rabinow and Sullivan, *Interpretive Social Science*, p. 46.

This is not to say that human beings are always fully cognizant of their participation in this on-going self-definition and self-interpretation process. Rather, in Giddens' terms, the activity of self-definition and self-interpretation often takes place at the level of 'practical consciousness' (and not the more explicitly self-conscious level of 'discursive consciousness'). See Anthony Giddens, *The Constitution of Society: Outline of the Theory of Structuration* (Cambridge: Polity Press, 1984), p. 375.

10 As was noted in the previous chapter.

11 Following Winch, Anthony Giddens has attempted to theorize the two levels at which social science is interpretive. See his discussion of the 'double hermeneutic' in *The Constitution of Society*, p. 374.

12 For example, the regularities in the interaction of molecules which serve as the focus of chemistry need not be considered in relation to any 'self-interpretations' or 'self-definitions' of those molecules.

13 Taylor, 'Interpretation and the Sciences of Man', p. 48.

14 'Interpretation and the Sciences of Man', p. 58.

15 'Interpretation and the Sciences of Man', p. 59.

16 *Ibid*.

17 *Ibid*.

As Taylor notes, one particularly promising way of conceptualizing 'intersubjective meanings', the full implications of which are beyond the scope of this book, is as 'rules' having both normative and constitutive effect. Once again, Anthony Giddens has made an important contribution in this regard. See his discussion of 'structuration theory' in *New Rules of Sociological Method: A Positive Critique of Interpretive Sociologies* (London: Hutchinson, 1976). For a useful discussion and critique of Giddens' contribution, see John B. Thompson, 'The Theory of Structuration', in David Held and John B. Thompson, eds., *Social Theory of Modern Societies:*

Anthony Giddens and His Critics (Cambridge: Cambridge University Press, 1989).

18 'Interpretation and the Sciences of Man', p. 57.
19 'Interpretation and the Sciences of Man', p. 52.
20 'Interpretation and the Sciences of Man', pp. 52–3.
21 Rabinow and Sullivan, 'The Interpretive Turn', p. 6.
22 *Ibid.*
23 *Ibid.* The work of Hans-Georg Gadamer has particular relevance to this point. For a good introduction to his work in this regard, see Georgia Warnke, *Gadamer: Hermeneutics, Tradition, and Reason* (Stanford, Calif.: Stanford University Press, 1987).
24 'The Interpretive Turn', p. 7. Rabinow and Sullivan are quoting Taylor. Or again, as Taylor notes,
> It is not just that all or most people in our society have a given set of ideas in their heads and subscribe to a given set of goals. The meanings and norms implicit in these practices are not just in the minds of the actors but are out there in the practices themselves, practices which cannot be conceived as a set of individual actions, but which are essentially modes of social relation, of mutual action.
> 'Interpretation and the Sciences of Man', pp. 56–7.
25 Taylor, 'Interpretation and the Sciences of Man', p. 43.
26 It should, of course, be emphasized that to 'make sense' of some behaviour in no way implies that the behaviour is rational. On the other hand, as Taylor notes, 'even contradictory, irrational action is 'made sense of', when we understand why it was engaged in'. 'Interpretation and the Sciences of Man', p. 43.
27 From the perspective of the 'hermeneutic circle', then, the proper analogy for the methodology of an interpretive approach is not the method of physics (the subsumption of empirical regularities under covering laws), nor that of Dilthey's 'romantic hermeneutics' (empathic identification), but rather the learning of a second language (the 'web of meaning' which constitutes observed social practices) and then the translation of that language into one's mother tongue (the concepts of the social scientist). For a discussion of hermeneutics not as 'empathy' but as a form of 'translation', see Hans-Georg Gadamer, *Truth and Method* (New York: Crossroad, 1988).
28 Though it might be argued that the formulations of some interpretive theorists – starting with Dilthey – have tended in this direction. For a critique of this more limited notion of an interpretive approach to the social world, see Brian Fay, *Social Theory and Political Practice* (London: George Allen & Unwin, 1975), chapter four. For a response which argues that Fay's critique does not apply to all forms of interpretive social science – in particular, to that proposed by Charles Taylor – see Michael Gibbons, 'Introduction: The Politics of Interpretation', in M. Gibbons, ed., *Interpreting Politics* (Oxford: Blackwell, 1987).

29 I have placed the word 'recovering' in inverted commas to underscore the problematic nature of the 'recovery' process. Specifically, the notion of 'recovering' the intersubjective meanings particular to a community of human agents is problematic for at least two reasons. First, though such meanings are always the product of an on-going process of self-interpretation and self-definition, as was noted above, that process is rarely one about which human agents are reflexively self-conscious. As a consequence, the human agents themselves may be incapable of articulating the 'intersubjective meanings' which constitute their prac-tices. To 'recover' unarticulated 'intersubjective meanings' is then no simple and straightforward activity.

Secondly, the notion of 'recovery' must also be nuanced through the recognition that all acts of 'recovery' involve interpretation. That is, the 'reading' of a specific 'web of meaning' and social practice is, in keeping with the reality of the 'double hermeneutic', expressed in the language and terms of the social scientist. And because there is no way to escape the 'hermeneutic circle' – because there is never any way to establish the validity of a particular reading beyond any doubt – every 'reading', no matter how plausible or sophisticated, remains potentially contestable.

In short, an interpretive approach does not alter in any way the sense in which a 'science' of international politics is 'interpretive' in the way that all scientific activity is 'interpretive' – i.e., all scientific activity involves the 'interpretation' of data in terms of paradigm-specific conventions about what constitutes 'valid knowledge'. In other words, the focus on the 'intersubjective meanings' which constitute social practices is no escape from the 'Cartesian anxiety' (see chapter three). For an argument which does advocate the incorporation of 'intersubjective meanings' into Interna-tional Relations theory as a means of getting around the problems posed by the paradigm-determined nature of all knowledge, see Roger Tooze, 'Economic Belief Systems and Understanding International Relations', in Richard Little and Steve Smith, eds., *Belief Systems and International Relations* (Oxford: Blackwell, 1988), pp. 132–3.

30 'Interpretation and the Sciences of Man', p. 59, my emphasis.

31 'Interpretation and the Sciences of Man', p. 46, my emphasis.

32 Because an interpretive approach focuses first and foremost on 'inter-subjective meanings', there is no difficulty in accommodating the need to examine, for example, unintended consequences of human behaviour or structural dimensions of human interaction (as there would be were 'subjective meanings' the exclusive focus).

It should be noted that although Taylor's work is being privileged in this chapter, contemporary interpretive social science draws on and has been influenced by at least five distinct traditions, including (i) the tradition of phenomenology/ethnomethodology as developed by Husserl and Schutz; (ii) the 'linguistic tradition' as developed by the later Wittgenstein and Winch (and into which Taylor's work falls); (iii) the hermeneutic tradition as developed by Heidegger and Gadamer; (iv) the tradition of Critical Theory as developed by Marx and Habermas; and (v) the tradition of genealogy as developed by Nietzsche and Foucault. Despite their differences, the five traditions do share the commonality of seeing the dimension of 'meaning' as both 'intersubjective' in nature and 'constitutive' of social reality. For useful introductions to the various traditions represented in contemporary interpretive social science, see Gibbons, *Interpreting Politics*, Dallmayr and McCarthy, *Understanding and Social Inquiry*, and Rabinow and Sullivan, *Interpretive Social Science*.

For a critical discussion of the distinctive characteristics of Taylor's approach – an approach Gibbons terms 'Critical-Expressivism' – see Gibbons, 'Introduction: The Politics of Interpretation', in Gibbons, *Interpreting Politics*. For an interesting comparison of this approach with that of genealogy, see Michael T. Gibbons, 'Interpretation, Genealogy and Human Agency', in Terence Ball, ed., *Idioms of Inquiry: Critique and Renewal in Political Science* (Albany: State University of New York Press, 1987).

33 Taylor, 'Interpretation and the Sciences of Man', p. 47.

For a good discussion of the place of the 'hermeneutics of recovery' in interpretive social science, see Michael Gibbons, 'Introduction', in Gibbons, *Interpreting Politics*.

34 *Politics Among Nations: The Struggle for Power and Peace*, 6th edn (New York: Knopf, 1985), p. 4.

35 *Politics Among Nations*, p. 5.

36 Richard K. Ashley, 'Political Realism and Human Interests', *International Studies Quarterly*, 25, No. 2 (1981), p. 207.

37 Ashley, 'Political Realism and Human Interests', pp. 209–10.

38 Jim George, 'The Study of International Relations and the Positivist/ Empiricist Theory of Knowledge', in R. Higgott, ed., *New Directions in International Relations? Australian Perspectives* (Canberra: The Australian National University, 1988), p. 93. See also Jim George, *Discourses of Global Politics: A Critical (Re)Introduction to International Relations* (Boulder: Lynne Rienner, 1994), pp. 172–6.

39 Michael Nicholson, who stands as one of the most sophisticated advocates of naturalism in the discipline, provides an excellent example of the positivistic incorporation of *Verstehen*. He notes that:

> A social scientist with a good empathetic understanding of his subject-matter is more likely to seize on goals which are fruitful than one who has little understanding of his subject. However, the empathy is a means to an end. The tests of goals are the indirect ones and empathy as such plays no part in the logic of the explanation, however large a part it played in suggesting the form of the explanation in the first place ... The test of empathy [*Verstehen*] is not its intensity but its predictions. It is a useful guide, but the discipline of testing must be given primacy.

M. Nicholson, *The Scientific Analysis of Social Behaviour* (London: Frances Pinter, 1983), pp. 60–61. See also M. Nicholson, *Rationality and the Analysis of International Conflict* (Cambridge: Cambridge University Press, 1992), esp. chapter 12.

40 In George's words, 'Morgenthau's realist theory is ... for all its hermeneutic posturing, finally constructed upon an empiricist theory of knowledge', where his 'Verstehen-based interpretivist perspectives ... are the other side of the positivist coin'. 'The Study of International Relations and the Positivist/Empiricist Theory of Knowledge', p. 94; *Discourses of Global Politics*, p. 176.

This is not to say that no evidence can be found in Morgenthau's work for a truly 'interpretive' approach to world politics: see note 74, below.

41 Morgenthau, *Politics Among Nations*, p. 4.

42 See John Vasquez, *The Power of Power Politics: A Critique* (New Brunswick, N.J.: Rutgers University Press, 1983).

43 For an overview of the literature of the early wave of systems theory, see Michael P. Sullivan, *International Relations: Theories and Evidence* (Englewood Cliffs, N.J.: Prentice-Hall, 1976), Part II. The most sophisticated and elegant contemporary contribution to 'systems theory' is, of course, Kenneth Waltz's *Theory of International Politics* (New York: Random House, 1979).

44 Steve Smith, 'Belief Systems and the Study of International Relations', in Little and Smith, *Belief Systems and International Relations*, p. 16.

45 Morgenthau, *Politics Among Nations*, p. 5, my emphasis.

46 'Strategic Beliefs, Mythology and Imagery', in Little and Smith, *Belief Systems and International Relations*, p. 140.

47 As Smith has noted, the dual focus of the discipline was manifest in Waltz's analysis of the causes of war, as well as serving as the subject of a classic article by Singer, in which he spoke of the 'level-of-analysis problem' in International Relations theory. See *Belief Systems and International Relations*, p. 16.

See also Kenneth Waltz, *Man, The State, and War: A Theoretical Analysis* (New York: Columbia University Press, 1959), and J. D. Singer, 'The Level of Analysis Problem in International Relations', in K. Knorr and S. Verba, eds., *The International System: Theoretical Essays* (Princeton, N.J.: Princeton University Press, 1961).

48 See Kenneth Boulding, *The Image: Knowledge in Life and Society* (Ann Arbor, Mich.: University of Michigan Press, 1956).

49 See Ole Holsti, 'The Belief System and National Images: A Case Study', *Journal of Conflict Resolution*, 6 (1962), pp. 244–52.

50 See Alexander George, 'The "Operational Code": A Neglected Approach to the Study of Political Leaders and Decision-Making', *International Studies Quarterly*, 13 (1969), pp. 190–222.

51 See Robert Axelrod, ed., *Structure of Decision* (Princeton, N.J.: Princeton University Press, 1976).

52 See Ernest May, *'Lessons' of the Past: The Use and Misuse of History in American Foreign Policy* (New York: Oxford University Press, 1973). See also, Ernest May and Richard Neustadt, *Thinking in Time* (New York: Free Press, 1986).

53 See Michael Brecher, Blema Steinberg and Janice Stein, 'A Framework for Research on Foreign Policy Behaviour', *Journal of Conflict Resolution*, 13, No. 1 (1969), pp. 75–101.

54 For an excellent overview of the distinctive characteristics of these different approaches and techniques, as well as references, see Smith, 'Belief Systems and the Study of International Relations', pp. 17–27.

55 The term is A. N. Oppenheim's. See his 'Psychological Processes in World Society', in Michael Banks, ed., *Conflict in World Society* (Brighton: Harvester, 1984), p. 114.

56 Smith, 'Belief Systems and the Study of International Relations', p. 11.

57 Smith, 'Belief Systems and the Study of International Relations', p. 16.

58 See Robert O. Keohane, 'International Institutions: Two Approaches', *International Studies Quarterly*, 32, No. 4 (1988), pp. 379–96. It should be noted that what in this essay are termed the 'interpretive' and 'positivist' approaches, Keohane refers to as 'reflective' and 'rationalist' approaches, respectively.

59 'International Institutions', p. 381, my emphasis. In addition to the interpretive efforts undertaken by Ruggie, Kratochwil, Alker, Ashley, Haas and Cox, one might also note those of Nicholas Onuf, Alexander Wendt, and Raymond Duvall. See Nicholas G. Onuf, *World of Our Making: Rules and Rule in Social Theory and International Relations* (Columbia, S.C.: University of South Carolina Press, 1989); Alexander Wendt, 'The Agent–Structure Problem in International Relations Theory', *International Organization*, 41, No. 3 (1987), pp. 335–70.

60 'International Institutions', p. 379.

61 Stephen D. Krasner, 'Structural Causes and Regime Consequences: Regimes as Intervening Variables', in S. Krasner, ed., *International Regimes* (Ithaca, N.Y.: Cornell University Press, 1983), p. 2. The definition continues:
    Principles are beliefs of fact, causation, and rectitude. Norms are standards of behaviour defined in terms of rights and obligations. Rules are specific prescriptions or proscriptions for action. Decision-making procedures are prevailing practices for making and implementing collective choice.

62 For a representative sampling, see Krasner, *International Regimes*, as well as Kenneth A. Oye, ed., *Cooperation Under Anarchy* (Princeton, N.J.: Princeton University Press, 1985).

63 Friedrich Kratochwil and John Gerard Ruggie, 'International Organization: A State of the Art on an Art of the State', *International Organization*, 40, No. 4 (1986), p. 764.

64 'International Organization', p. 771. Nor are they daunted by predictable attempts by at least some members of the International Relations community to discredit interpretive approaches, (p. 765):

> Interpretive epistemologies that stress the intimate relationship between validation and the uncovering of intersubjective meanings are simply too well developed today to be easily dismissed by charges of subjectivism – or, more likely in the arena of international relations theory, of idealism.

65 For example, Kratochwil and Ruggie argue that by treating the norms which are an integral part of regimes as intersubjective elements of a 'web of meaning' which form the 'constitutive basis of regimes' – instead of the more common practice of treating them as 'causal variables' determining behaviour – regimes can be seen to be vibrant and robust even when norms are ignored in specific instances. See the discussion by Kratochwil in 'Regimes, Interpretation and the 'Science' of Politics: A Reappraisal', *Millennium*, 17, No. 2 (1988), pp. 277–8.

Similarly, they argue that recognizing the intersubjective nature of the 'principles', 'norms', etc. which constitute regimes as social practices (and not as timeless behavioural regularities) also provides a means of theorizing the change within and of regimes. In short, regimes are subject to change because they are the product of an on-going process of community self-interpretation and self-definition in response to changing context. As such, an interpretive approach to the study of regimes avoids positivism's problematic assumption that 'once the machinery is in place, actors merely remain programmed by it'. 'International Organization', p. 770.

It is lamentable – if not surprising given the traditional antipathy in the discipline to meta-theoretical questions – that in a recent reprinting of Kratochwil and Ruggie's 'International Organization' the discussion of the need for interpretive methodologies has been deleted. See Paul F. Diehl, ed., *The Politics of International Organizations: Patterns and Insights* (Chicago: Dorsey Press, 1989), pp. 17–27.

66 Kratochwil and Ruggie, 'International Organization', p. 774.

67 Nor is this the only difficulty in their treatment of interpretive social science. Even as they are promoting interpretive social science as a distinct alternative to positivism, for example, the formulation of regimes as intersubjective in nature because they involve 'converging expectations' comes dangerously close to confusing the important distinction, noted earlier by Taylor, between intersubjective meanings and consensus in terms of subjective meanings. Similarly, in an earlier piece, Kratochwil seems to link an interpretive approach to an analysis of the 'background of intentions', rather than the intersubjective meanings which make subjective intentions possible in the first place. See Friedrich Kratochwil, 'Errors have their advantage', *International Organization*, 38, No. 2 (1984), p. 319. It should be noted that Kratochwil has revised his position in a

fashion more in line with interpretive social science in more recent contributions.

68 For example, liberal trade and monetary regimes.

69 Martin Hollis and Steve Smith, *Explaining and Understanding International Relations* (Oxford: Clarendon Press, 1990).

70 A formulation with strong affinities to that of Charles Taylor.

71 *Explaining and Understanding International Relations*, p. 179.

72 *Explaining and Understanding International Relations*, p. 180.

73 *Ibid.*

74 It is even possible that with this latest turn in neorealist theory, there may be hope for a rediscovery and revaluation of the contributions of those classical realists who – in contrast to neorealists – saw even conflictual, coercive forms of state interaction such as the 'balance of power' as 'social institutions', comprised of rules and roles, and serving to regulate the conflict-prone 'anarchical society' of states. The contribution of Hedley Bull – in particular, his *The Anarchical Society: A Study of Order in World Politics* (New York: Columbia University Press, 1977) – is perhaps the prime example here, though one might read Morgenthau's comments on balance of power as a moral consensus (*Politics Among Nations*, chapter 14) as an attempt to draw attention to the intersubjective meanings underlying the practices which together comprise the 'balance of power'.

75 We are reminded here of Martin Wight's affirmation, in a formulation having obvious affinity with the positivist assumption of naturalism, that international politics is 'the realm of recurrence and repetition'; 'the field in which political action is most regularly necessitous'. Martin Wight, 'Why is There No International Theory?' in H. Butterfield and M. Wight, eds., *Diplomatic Investigations: Essays in the Theory of International Politics* (London: George Allen & Unwin, 1966), p. 26. On naturalism, see chapter two above.

76 Oran R. Young, *International Cooperation: Building Regimes for Natural Resources and the Environment* (Ithaca: Cornell University Press, 1989), p. 14.

77 In this sense, interpretive social science must be seen as standing in a 'relational contradiction' to the realist tradition; as being both 'life-giving' (in providing realism with a way of overcoming anomalies in the study of regimes) as well as 'life-taking' (in undermining realism's foundational 'myth' of the essentially unchanging and self-reproducing nature of international politics). On the notion of 'relational contradictions' as simultaneously 'life-giving' and 'life-taking', as both sustaining and undermining, see Robert L. Heilbroner, *Marxism: For and Against* (New York: W. W. Norton & Co., 1980), chapter two.

78 Robert W. Cox, 'Social Forces, States and World Orders: Beyond International Relations Theory', in Robert O. Keohane, ed., *Neorealism and Its Critics* (New York: Columbia University Press, 1986), p. 218.

79 See Richard K. Ashley, 'Living on the Border Lines: Man, Poststructuralism and War', in James Der Derian and Michael J. Shapiro, eds., *International/Intertextual Relations: Postmodern Readings of World Politics* (Toronto: Lexington Books, 1989); Richard K. Ashley, 'Untying the Sovereign State: A Double Reading of the Anarchy Problematique', *Millennium*, 17 (1988), pp. 227–62; and David Campbell, *Writing Security: United States' Foreign Policy and the Politics of Identity* (Manchester: Manchester University Press, 1992), respectively. For a useful introduction and overview to the contributions of these postmodernists and others, see Jim George, *Discourses of Global Politics*, especially chapter eight.

80 The notion of gender as 'packages of expectations' is Cynthia Enloe's . See her path-breaking work, *Bananas, Beaches and Bases: Making Feminist Sense of International Politics* (London: Pandora, 1989), as well as her more recent *The Morning After: Sexual Politics At the End of the Cold War* (Berkeley: University of California Press, 1993). See also Sandra Whitworth, *Feminism and International Relations* (London: Macmillan, 1994).

In a related vein, Jean Elshtain's *Women and War* (New York: Basic Books, 1987) explores the intersubjective meanings associated with the ethic of 'armed civic virtue', and the attendant gendered identities of men – (public) 'just warriors' – and women – (private) 'beautiful souls' – bequeathed to Western moderns. For a critique which argues that while Elshtain's work serves to underscore the socially constructed *reception* of gender differences, it does not adequately address the social construction of gender as difference, see Sarah Brown, 'Feminism, International Theory, and International Relations of Gender Inequality', *Millennium*, 17, No. 3 (1988), pp. 461–75.

81 Of course, while the possibility of fundamental change may serve as an antidote to positivist/realist-inspired pessimism about the possibility of progress – a pessimism grounded in the assumption of the essentially unchanging (and unchangeable) nature of international politics – it is not sufficient, in and of itself, to dispel all forms of pessimism. For example, it is quite possible to accept the potential for changing existing social practices while maintaining that efforts to effect progress through change of social practices inevitably make things worse. Similarly, one can argue that the recognition of the possibility of change does not, on its own, necessarily lead to emancipation, in that the latter also requires an independent, normative judgment about the way the world should be.

82 Jürgen Habermas, *Knowledge and Human Interests*, trans. Jeremy J. Shapiro (Boston: Beacon Press, 1971), p. 310.

83 'International Institutions', p. 381.

84 On the distinction between 'traditional' and 'critical' theory, see Max Horkheimer, 'Traditional and Critical Theory', in Horkheimer, *Critical Theory: Selected Essays* (New York: Continuum, 1989), pp. 188–243. What

Horkheimer calls 'traditional theory', Cox terms 'problem-solving theory'. See chapter three above.

85 It is ironic, in this regard, that one of the most insightful analyses of the way intersubjective meanings constitute not only regulatory institutions within the global order but the global order itself is to be found in Ruggie's discussion of the shift from the medieval to the modern world system. See John Gerard Ruggie, 'Continuity and Transformation in the World Polity: Toward a Neorealist Synthesis', in Keohane, *Neorealism and Its Critics*, pp. 131–57. It is not clear how Ruggie reconciles his historicist sensitivity with the reification of the state/inter-state system that his realism would seem to require, and that his meta-theoretical pronouncements on the appropriate subject matter of interpretively oriented analysis reinforce.

86 This concern can be seen quite clearly, for example, in Cox's Gramscian-inspired efforts to develop an historicist approach which focuses on the intersubjective meanings which predominate in a given context, and how changes in those meanings give rise to changes in global order. Although a full discussion of Cox's conception of hegemony in international politics is beyond the scope of this study, it is significant that what distinguishes it from the positivist-inspired neorealist conception of hegemony is that Cox's Gramscian notion of hegemony 'joins an ideological and inter-subjective element to the brute power relationship'. 'Postscript 1985', in Keohane, *Neorealism and Its Critics*, p. 246. See also Cox, 'Gramsci, Hegemony and International Relations: An Essay in Method, *Millennium*, 12, No. 2 (1983), pp. 162–75.

87 It is important to recognize, moreover, that the change in intersubjective meanings which is the product of the on-going process of collective self-interpretation and self-definition cannot be equated with a change in subjective 'preferences', as is suggested by Keohane. Subjective preferences may indeed change, but such a change would not result in a fundamental change as would be the case of change in intersubjective meanings of which subjective preferences are derivative. As such, Keohane's formulation of intersubjectivity as 'preferences' indicates again the difficulties experienced by mainstream, positivist-inspired theorists in comprehending the nature of the interpretivist challenge. See Keohane, 'International Institutions', p. 391.

88 For example, Robert Keohane, operating from a Lakatosian positivist position, faults interpretive approaches for their failure to develop an adequate 'research program that could be employed by students of world politics'. 'Waltzian neorealism', he notes,

> has such a research program; so does neoliberal institutionalism, which has focused on the evolution and impact of international regimes. Until the reflective [i.e., interpretive] scholars or others sympathetic to their arguments have delineated such a research program and shown in particular studies that it can illuminate important issues in world politics, they will remain on the margins of the field, largely invisible to the preponderance of empirical

researchers, most of whom explicitly or implicitly accept one or another versions of rationalistic [i.e., positivistic] premises.

'International Institutions', p. 392.

For an 'interpretivist' response to and criticism of Keohane's positivistically informed discussion of interpretive approaches to international politics, see R. B. J. Walker, 'History and Structure in the Theory of International Studies', *Millennium*, 18, No. 2 (1989).

5 International Relations theory and social criticism

1 'The Nature and Limits of a Theory of International Relations', in William T. R. Fox, ed., *Theoretical Aspects of International Relations* (Notre Dame, Ind.: University of Notre Dame Press, 1959), p. 18.

2 *One-Dimensional Man* (Boston: Beacon Press, 1964), p. 156, emphasis in the original.

3 Steve Smith, 'The Forty Years' Detour: The Resurgence of Normative Theory in International Relations', *Millennium*, 21, No. 3 (1992), p. 489.

4 'Thinking Theory Thoroughly', in *The Scientific Study of Foreign Policy*, rev. edn (London: Frances Pinter, 1980), p. 22.

It is clear that Rosenau defines the idea of a scientific theory of International Relations in terms of the positivist tradition: 'To think theoretically', he affirms, 'one must be able to assume that human affairs are founded on an underlying order', and 'one must be predisposed to ask about every event, every situation, or every observed phenomenon, "Of what is it an instance?"' (p. 25).

5 'Thinking Theory Thoroughly', p. 22.

6 *Ibid.*

7 *Ibid.*

8 'Thinking Theory Thoroughly', p. 23.

9 'Thinking Theory Thoroughly', p. 22.

10 'Thinking Theory Thoroughly', p. 23.

11 *Ibid.*

12 *Ibid.*

Of course, Rosenau is not alone in this regard. Kal Holsti, for example, clearly indicates his acceptance of the positivist tenet of the 'value-free' nature of scientific knowledge in his castigation of the World Order Models Project (WOMP) for engaging in a normatively based condemnation of the nation-state system which 'does little to enhance international theory as a discipline with scientific pretensions'. See Holsti, *The Dividing Discipline: Hegemony and Diversity in International Theory* (Boston: Allen & Unwin, 1985), p. 141.

13 Richard J. Bernstein, *The Restructuring of Social and Political Theory* (New York: Harcourt Brace Jovanovich, 1976), p. 54.

14 See his *Formal Theories in International Relations* (Cambridge: Cambridge University Press, 1989), as well as his *Rationality and the Analysis of International Conflict* (Cambridge: Cambridge University Press, 1992).

15 Michael Nicholson, *The Scientific Analysis of Social Behaviour* (London: Frances Pinter, 1983). Accordingly, it will be this earlier work which will be the focus here.

16 *Scientific Analysis*, p. 6.

17 *Scientific Analysis*, p. 9.

18 *Scientific Analysis*, p. 5.

19 *Scientific Analysis*, p. 235.

20 *Scientific Analysis*, p. 236.

21 *Scientific Analysis*, p. 237.

22 *Scientific Analysis*, p. 235.

23 *Scientific Analysis*, p. 9.

24 *Scientific Analysis*, p. 244.

25 *Scientific Analysis*, p. 9.

26 Mervyn Frost, *Towards a Normative Theory of International Relations* (Cambridge: Cambridge University Press, 1986), p. 2.

27 *Towards a Normative Theory*, p. 16.

28 Brian Fay, *Social Theory and Political Practice* (London: George Allen & Unwin, 1975), p. 40.

29 *Ibid.*, emphasis in the original.

30 Fay, *Social Theory and Political Practice*, pp. 40–1.

31 As quoted in Fay, *Social Theory and Political Practice*, p. 37.

32 *One-Dimensional Man*, pp. 153–4.

33 *One-Dimensional Man*, p. 146.

34 Jürgen Habermas, 'The Scientization of Politics and Public Opinion', in Habermas, *Toward a Rational Society*, trans. Jeremy J. Shapiro (Boston: Beacon Press, 1970), pp. 63–64.

35 *One-Dimensional Man*, pp. 158–9.

36 *Scientific Analysis*, p. 3.

37 *Scientific Analysis*, p. 235.

38 *Scientific Analysis*, p. 244.

   Nor is Nicholson alone in this regard. 'The urge to explain', notes Waltz, 'is not born of idle curiosity alone. It is produced also by the *desire to control, or at least to know if control is possible'. Theory of International Politics* (New York: Random House, 1979), p. 6, my emphasis.

   The same 'control-impulse' is to be found in positivistically oriented 'peace research', particularly as post-behaviouralist concerns with 'relevance' and 'action' have taken centre-stage. As two critical peace researchers have noted:

   For more and more peace researchers, the chasm between peace research and peace action, between peace researcher as knower and the peace researcher as actor, has come to be regarded as a particularly acute problem. Some (like Lentz and the Newcombes) have redoubled their efforts to devise more sophisticated *technical means and instrumental strategies* for predicting and/or repressing the outbreak of violence.

157

Herbert G. Reid and Ernest J. Yanarella, 'Toward a Critical Theory of Peace Research in the United States: the Search for an "Intelligible Core"', *Journal of Peace Research*, 13, No. 4 (1976), p. 331, emphasis added.

39 Bernstein, *The Restructuring of Social and Political Theory*, pp. 52–3.

40 'The Poverty of Neorealism', in Robert O. Keohane, ed., *Neorealism and Its Critics* (New York: Columbia University Press, 1986), p. 292.

41 *Ibid.*

42 'The Poverty of Neorealism', p. 258, my emphasis.

Once again, it is important to be clear about what is being argued. To the extent that neorealism feeds into a 'totalitarian project', it does so not because it is *realist* but because it is *positivist*. A liberal/pluralist or radical approach to international politics, for example, despite the significant differences from one which is realist in inspiration, also contributes to a politics of 'domination' to the extent that it is positivist.

43 R. B. J. Walker, 'History and Structure in the Theory of International Studies', *Millennium*, 18, No. 2 (1989), p. 163, my emphasis.

44 Robert W. Cox, 'Social Forces, States and World Orders: Beyond International Relations Theory', in Keohane, *Neorealism and Its Critics*, pp. 208, 210.

45 Frost, *Towards a Normative Theory*, p. 2.

46 See, for example, Terry Nardin and David R. Mapel, eds., *Traditions of International Ethics* (Cambridge: Cambridge University Press, 1992), as well as Chris Brown, *International Relations Theory: New Normative Approaches* (London: Wheatsheaf, 1992).

47 See his *International Relations Theory*.

48 Brown, *International Relations Theory*, p. 3. Brown, however, and in contrast to Nicholson, provides no arguments in support of this position. A pessimistic reading would suggest that in the time period between Nicholson's and Brown's interventions, the distinction between normative and empirical theorizing has come to be viewed as sufficiently uncontroversial as to make further justifications unnecessary.

49 Nardin and Mapel (*Traditions of International Ethics*) do not take up the issue at all. Brown notes the impetus for normative theory in the 'postbehavioural revolution' – that is, the concern for 'relevance' borne of the 'sudden discovery by American social scientists that they had been ignoring the real problems of American society' (*International Relations Theory*, p. 9). Unfortunately he does not investigate the implications for the role of normative International Relations theory implicit in postbehaviouralism's positivist accommodation of 'normative' to 'non-normative' theory.

50 Nicholson, *Scientific Analysis*, p. 235. Rosenau promotes the same kind of understanding of the proper relationship between 'normative' and 'non-normative' empirical theory. To overcome students' resistance to separating fact and value, Rosenau suggests the following:

This is the one line of reasoning on behalf of thinking theoretically that my most value-committed students find persuasive. If empirical theory is posited as a tool of moral theory, they can approach it instrumentally and see virtue in habituating themselves to distinguishing between the two.

'Thinking Theory Thoroughly', p. 22.

51 Smith, 'The Forty Years' Detour', p. 490.
52 James Rosenau, 'Thinking Theory Thoroughly', p. 22, my emphasis.
53 (Boulder: Lynne Rienner, 1993).
54 *Politics Without Principle*, p. 3.
55 *Politics Without Principle*, p. 91.
56 *Politics Without Principle*, p. 92.
57 *Ibid.*
58 *Ibid.*, emphasis in the original.
59 *Politics Without Principle*, p. 93.
60 *Ibid.* The term is that of Emmanuel Levinas.
61 *Politics Without Principle*, p. 94.
62 *Politics Without Principle*, pp. 95, 97, 94.
63 Richard K. Ashley and R. B. J. Walker, 'Speaking the Language of Exile: Dissident Thought in International Studies', *International Studies Quarterly*, 34, No. 3 (1990), p. 260.
64 Richard K. Ashley and R. B. J. Walker, 'Reading Dissidence/Writing the Discipline: Crisis and the Question of Sovereignty in International Studies', *International Studies Quarterly*, 34, No. 3 (1990), p. 391.
65 See R. B. J. Walker, *One World, Many Worlds: Struggles for a Just World Peace* (Boulder: Lynne Rienner, 1988). For a useful overview, see Jim George, *Discourses of Global Politics: A Critical (Re)Introduction to International Relations* (Boulder: Lynne Rienner, 1994), chapter eight.
66 George, *Discourses of Global Politics*, p. 212, emphasis in the original.
67 Walker, *One World, Many Worlds*, p. 160. Also quoted in George, *Discourses of Global Politics*, p. 215.
68 Richard J. Bernstein, *The New Constellation: The Ethical–Political Horizons of Modernity/Postmodernity* (Cambridge: Polity Press, 1991), p. 51. It is the exclusionary dimension of the celebrated 'conversation of mankind' that explains why postmodernist theorists like Derrida and Foucault 'speak' (pp. 51–2)

to those who have felt the pain and suffering of being excluded by the prevailing hierarchies in the text called 'the history of the West' – whether they be women, Blacks, or others bludgeoned by the exclusionary tactics.

69 Bernstein, *The New Constellation*, p. 163.
70 M. Foucault, *Power, Truth, Strategy* (Sydney: Feral Publications, 1979), p. 35, quoted in Richard K. Ashley, 'The Geopolitics of Geopolitical Space: Toward a Critical Social Theory of International Politics', *Alternatives*, 12, No. 4 (1987), p. 408, emphasis added.
71 Ashley, 'The Geopolitics of Geopolitical Space', p. 410.

72 *Politics Without Principle*, p. 91.
73 Michael T. Gibbons, 'Interpretation, Genealogy, and Human Agency', in Terence Ball, ed., *Idioms of Inquiry: Critique and Renewal in Political Science* (Albany: State University of New York Press, 1987), p. 161.
74 A tradition exemplified by theorists such as Charles Taylor.
75 Gibbons, 'Interpretation, Genealogy, and Human Agency', p. 161.
76 *Ibid.*
77 Gibbons, 'Interpretation, Genealogy, and Human Agency', p. 162.
78 'Reading Dissidence', p. 391.
79 Jim George and David Campbell, 'Patterns of Dissent and the Celebration of Difference: Critical Social Theory and International Relations', *International Studies Quarterly*, 34, No. 3 (1990), p. 281.
80 'Reading Dissidence', p. 391.
81 For a good overview, see Georgia Warnke, *Justice and Interpretation* (Cambridge: Polity Press, 1992).
82 Bernstein, *The New Constellation*, p. 160, emphasis in the original.
83 'Discourse Analysis: Teaching World Politics Through International Relations', in Lev S. Gonick and Edward Weisband, eds., *Teaching World Politics: Contending Pedagogies for a New World Order* (Boulder: Westview Press, 1992), p. 166.
84 'Ethics, Modernity, Community', in Walker, *Inside/Outside: International Relations as Political Theory* (Cambridge: Cambridge University Press, 1993), p. 77.
85 *One World, Many Worlds*, pp. 78–9.
86 *One World, Many Worlds*, p. 135.
87 See, for example, Seyla Benhabib, *Situating the Self: Gender, Community and Postmodernism in Contemporary Ethics* (New York: Routledge, 1992), as well as Bernstein, *The New Constellation*.
88 Gibbons, 'Interpretation, Genealogy, and Human Agency', p. 163.
89 See Gibbons, 'Interpretation, Genealogy, and Human Agency', pp. 155, 162–3, as well as Michel Foucault, 'Governability', *Ideology and Consciousness*, 6 (1979), 19.
90 'Thinking Theory Thoroughly', p. 22. He concludes by lamenting that 'often their empirical analyses *slip into moral judgments without their being aware of it*' (my emphasis). Given the widespread lack of awareness in the discipline of positivism's own normative content, this is a rather ironic observation.
91 See Gonick and Weisband, *Teaching World Politics*, p. 2.
92 The phrase is a clear reference to Nicholas Onuf's book of the same title (Columbia, S.C.: University of South Carolina Press, 1989).
93 Brian Fay, *Critical Social Science: Liberation and its Limits* (Cambridge: Polity Press, 1987), p. 89.
94 Frost refers to this as the 'democratic dimension of critical understanding'. See *Towards a Normative Theory*, p. 35. Significantly, Nicholson regards education as a 'form of social engineering'. See *Scientific Analysis*, p. 244.

95 It is lamentable that Freire's work would seem to have had relatively little impact on the discipline of International Relations. Indeed, even in contributions by members of the discipline on the subject of pedagogy, one sees only the scarcest of references to his arguments. For a rather atypical exploration of Freire's work in terms of war and peace issues, see Marguerite Rivage-Seul, 'Peace Education: Imagination and the Pedagogy of the Oppressed', *Harvard Educational Review*, 57, No. 2 (1987), pp. 153–69.

For an excellent critical introduction to and review of Freire's contribution to emancipatory pedagogy, see Stephen T. Leonard, *Critical Theory in Political Practice* (Princeton N.J.: Princeton University Press, 1990), chapter five.

96 One of the most common operationalizations of this strategy is that of the in-class 'simulation exercise'. Here, typically, students are asked to take on the identities of 'international actors' – e.g., diplomats, government officials, officers of international organizations – and to engage in mock international-type activities (e.g., inter-state negotiations to resolve a 'crisis'). For a critique of simulation exercises in terms of the two pedagogical strategies under discussion, see M. Neufeld, 'The Pedagogical is Political: The "Why", the "What", and the "How" in the Teaching of World Politics', in Gonick and Weisband, *Teaching World Politics*, chapter five.

97 Paulo Freire, *Pedagogy of the Oppressed* (New York: Continuum, 1983), p. 58.

98 Freire, *Pedagogy of the Oppressed*, p. 59.

99 *Ibid.*

100 *Pedagogy of the Oppressed*, p. 61.

101 Nancy Fraser, 'What's Critical about Critical Theory?' in Seyla Benhabib and Drucilla Cornell, eds., *Feminism as Critique.* (Minneapolis: University of Minnesota Press, 1986), p. 31.

102 Freire, *Pedagogy of the Oppressed*, p. 56.

103 Cynthia Enloe, *Bananas, Beaches and Bases: Making Feminist Sense of International Politics* (London: Pandora, 1989). For a representative example of a feminist pedagogy in world politics, see Anne Sisson Runyan, 'Undisciplining World Politics: The Personal is Political', in Gonick and Weisband, *Teaching World Politics*.

104 A particularly useful reading on this point is Bernice R. Sandler, 'The Classroom Climate: Chilly for Women?' in A. Deneef, C. Goodwin, and E. McCrate, eds., *The Academic's Handbook* (London: Duke University Press, 1988).

105 On this, see Enloe, *Bananas, Beaches and Bases*, chapter eight.

106 An interest which, as Aronowitz and Giroux note, must incorporate an 'engagement in self-criticism as a way to improve their own pedagogy and to signal their anti-authoritarian intention'. See Stanley Aronowitz and Henry Giroux, 'Radical Education and Transformative Intellectuals', *Canadian Journal of Political and Social Theory*, 19, No. 3 (1985), p. 56.

6 Conclusion

1 'The Nature and Limits of a Theory of International Relations', in William T. R. Fox, ed., *Theoretical Aspects of International Relations* (Notre Dame, Ind.: University of Notre Dame Press, 1959), p. 22.

2 Quoted in David Held, *Introduction to Critical Theory: Horkheimer to Habermas* (Berkeley: University of California Press, 1980), p. 192, emphasis in the original.

3 Karl Deutsch, *The Analysis of International Relations*, 3rd edn (Englewood Cliffs, N.J.: Prentice-Hall, 1988), p. ix.

4 'Traditionelle und Kritische Theorie', in Alfred Schmidt, ed., *Kritische Theorie: Eine Dokumentation* (Frankfurt: S. Fischer Verlag, 1968), I, p. 190, my translation.

5 For an excellent treatment of this dimension of critical forms of theorizing, see Stephen T. Leonard, *Critical Theory in Political Practice* (Princeton, N.J.: Princeton University Press, 1990).

6 Morgenthau, 'The Nature and Limits', p. 22.

7 *Ibid.*

Bibliography

Adorno, Theodor. *Negative Dialectics*. Trans. E. B. Ashton. New York: Continuum, 1973

Alker, Hayward R., Jr, and Thomas J. Biersteker. 'The Dialectics of World Order: Notes for a Future Archaeologist of International Savoir Faire'. *International Studies Quarterly*, 28, No. 2 (1984), 121–42

Arendt, Hannah. *The Human Condition*. Chicago: University of Chicago Press, 1958

On Revolution. New York: Viking Press, 1963

Aronowitz, Stanley, and Henry Giroux. 'Radical Education and Transformative Intellectuals'. *Canadian Journal of Political and Social Theory*, 19, No. 3 (1985), 48–63

Ashley, Richard K. 'Political Realism and Human Interests'. *International Studies Quarterly*, 25, No. 2 (1981), 204–36

'The Poverty of Neorealism'. In Robert O. Keohane, ed. *Neorealism and Its Critics*. New York: Columbia University Press, 1986

'The Geopolitics of Geopolitical Space: Toward a Critical Social Theory of International Politics'. *Alternatives*, 12, No. 4 (1987), 403–34

'Untying the Sovereign State: A Double Reading of the Anarchy Problematique'. *Millennium*, 17 (1988), 227–62

Ashley, Richard K., and R. B. J. Walker. 'Speaking the Language of Exile: Dissident Thought in International Studies'. *International Studies Quarterly*, 34, No. 3 (1990), 259–68

'Reading Dissidence/Writing the Discipline: Crisis and the Question of Sovereignty in International Studies'. *International Studies Quarterly*, 34, No. 3 (1990), 367–416

Avineri, Shlomo. *Hegel's Theory of the Modern State*. London: Cambridge University Press, 1972

Axelrod, Robert, ed. *Structure of Decision*. Princeton, N.J.: Princeton University Press, 1976

Banks, Michael. 'The Inter-Paradigm Debate'. In Margot Light and A. J. R. Groom, eds. *International Relations: A Handbook of Current Theory*. London: Pinter, 1985

163

Bibliography

Banks, Michael, ed. *Conflict in World Society*. Brighton: Harvester, 1984
Bechtel, William. *Philosophy of Science*. London: Lawrence Erlbaum, 1988
Benhabib, Seyla. *Situating the Self: Gender, Community and Postmodernism in Contemporary Ethics*. New York: Routledge, 1992
Bernstein, Richard J. *The Restructuring of Social and Political Theory*. New York: Harcourt Brace Jovanovich, 1976
   Beyond Objectivism and Relativism: Science, Hermeneutics, and Praxis. Philadelphia: University of Pennsylvania Press, 1983
   The New Constellation: The Ethical–Political Horizons of Modernity/Postmodernity. Cambridge: Polity Press, 1991
Boulding, Kenneth. *The Image: Knowledge in Life and Society*. Ann Arbor, Mich.: University of Michigan Press, 1956
Brecher, Michael, Blema Steinberg, and Janice Stein. 'A Framework for Research on Foreign Policy Behaviour'. *Journal of Conflict Resolution*, 13, No. 1 (1969), 75–101
Brown, Chris. *International Relations Theory: New Normative Approaches*. London: Wheatsheaf, 1992
Brown, Sarah. 'Feminism, International Theory, and International Relations of Gender Inequality'. *Millennium*, 17, No. 3 (1988), 461–75
Bull, Hedley. *The Anarchical Society: A Study of Order in World Politics*. New York: Columbia University Press, 1977
Campbell, David. *Writing Security: United States' Foreign Policy and the Politics of Identity*. Manchester: Manchester University Press, 1992
   Politics Without Principle: Sovereignty, Ethics and the Narratives of the Gulf War. Boulder: Lynne Rienner, 1993
Carr, E. H. *The Twenty-Years' Crisis, 1919–1939: An Introduction to the Study of International Relations*. London: Macmillan, 1939
Catlin, George E. G. *A Study of the Principles of Politics*. London: Allen & Unwin, 1930
Chalmers, A. F. *What is This Thing Called Science?* 2nd edn: St Lucia, Queensland: University of Queensland Press, 1982
Connerton, Paul, ed. *Critical Sociology: Selected Readings*. New York: Penguin, 1976
Connolly, William. 'Theoretical Self-Consciousness'. In William Connolly and Glen Gordon, eds. *Social Structure and Political Theory*. London: D. C. Heath, 1974
Cox, Robert W. 'Gramsci, Hegemony and International Relations: An Essay in Method'. *Millennium*, 12, No. 2 (1983), 162–75
   'Social Forces, States and World Orders: Beyond International Relations Theory' and 'Postscript 1985'. In Robert O. Keohane, ed. *Neorealism and Its Critics*. New York: Columbia University Press, 1986
Dahl, Robert. *Modern Political Analysis*. Englewood Cliffs, N.J.: Prentice-Hall, 1963
Dallmayr, Fred R. *Language and Politics*. Notre Dame, Ind.: University of Notre Dame Press, 1984

Dallmayr, Fred R., and Thomas A. McCarthy, eds. *Understanding and Social Inquiry*. Notre Dame, Ind.: University of Notre Dame Press, 1977

Der Derian, James. *On Diplomacy: A Genealogy of Western Estrangement*. Oxford: Basil Blackwell, 1987

Der Derian, James, and Michael J. Shapiro, eds. *International/Intertextual Relations: Postmodern Readings of World Politics*. Toronto: Lexington Books, 1989

Deutsch, Karl. *The Analysis of International Relations*. 3rd edn. Englewood Cliffs, N.J.: Prentice-Hall, 1988

Dictionary of Marxist Thought. Ed. Tom Bottomore. Cambridge, Mass.: Harvard University Press, 1983

Dictionary of Sociology. 2nd edn. Eds. Nicholas Abercrombie, Stephen Hill and Bryan S. Turner. London: Penguin Books, 1988

Diehl, Paul F., ed. *The Politics of International Organizations: Patterns and Insights*. Chicago: Dorsey Press, 1989

Easton, David. *The Political System: An Inquiry into the State of Political Science*. 2nd edn. New York: Alfred A. Knopf, 1971

Elshtain, Jean. *Women and War*. New York: Basic Books, 1987

Enloe, Cynthia. *Bananas, Beaches and Bases: Making Feminist Sense of International Politics*. London: Pandora, 1989

　The Morning After: Sexual Politics at the End of the Cold War. Berkeley: University of California Press, 1993

Falk, Richard. 'Anarchism and World Order'. *Nomos*, 19 (1978), 63–90

　The End of World Order: Essays on Normative International Relations. New York: Holmes & Meier, 1983

Fay, Brian. *Social Theory and Political Practice*. London: George Allen & Unwin, 1975

　Critical Social Science: Liberation and Its Limits. Cambridge: Polity Press, 1987

Ferguson, Yale H., and Richard W. Mansbach. *The Elusive Quest: Theory and International Politics*. Columbia, S.C.: University of South Carolina Press, 1988

Feyerabend, Paul. *Against Method: Outline of an Anarchistic Theory of Knowledge*. New York: New Left Books, 1975

Foucault, Michel. 'Governability', *Ideology and Consciousness*, 6 (1979), 19

Fraser, Nancy. 'What's Critical about Critical Theory?' In Seyla Benhabib and Drucilla Cornell, eds. *Feminism as Critique*. Minneapolis: University of Minnesota Press, 1986

Freire, Paulo. *Pedagogy of the Oppressed*. New York: Continuum, 1983

Frost, Mervyn. *Towards a Normative Theory of International Relations*. Cambridge: Cambridge University Press, 1986

Gadamer, Hans-Georg. *Truth and Method*. New York: Crossroad, 1988

Gareau, Fred. 'The Long, Uncertain Road to Social Science Maturity'. *International Journal of Cognitive Sociology*, 29, No. 3–4 (1988), 175–85

George, Alexander. 'The "Operational Code": A Neglected Approach to the Study of Political Leaders and Decision-Making'. *International Studies Quarterly*, 13, No. 2 (1969), 190–222

George, Jim. *Discourses of Global Politics: A Critical (Re)Introduction to International Relations*. Boulder: Lynne Rienner, 1994

George, Jim, and David Campbell. 'Patterns of Dissent and the Celebration of Difference: Critical Social Theory and International Relations'. *International Studies Quarterly*, 34, No. 3 (1990), 269–94

Germino, Dante. *Beyond Ideology: The Revival of Political Theory*. New York: Harper and Row, 1967

Gibbons, Michael T. 'Interpretation, Genealogy and Human Agency'. In Terence Ball, ed. *Idioms of Inquiry: Critique and Renewal in Political Science*. Albany: State University of New York Press, 1987

Gibbons, Michael, ed. *Interpreting Politics*. Oxford: Blackwell, 1987

Giddens, Anthony. *New Rules of Sociological Method: A Positive Critique of Interpretive Sociologies*. London: Hutchinson, 1976

   The Constitution of Society: Outline of the Theory of Structuration. Cambridge: Polity Press, 1984

Gill, Stephen, ed. *Gramsci, Historical Materialism and International Relations*. Cambridge: Cambridge University Press, 1993

Gilpin, Robert. *The Political Economy of International Relations*. Princeton, N.J.: Princeton University Press, 1987

Gonick, Lev S., and Edward Weisband, eds. *Teaching World Politics: Contending Pedagogies for a New World Order*. Boulder: Westview Press, 1992

Habermas, Jürgen. *Strukturwandel der Öffentlichkeit*. Berlin: Luchterhand, 1962

   Toward a Rational Society. Trans. Jeremy J. Shapiro. Boston: Beacon Press, 1970

   Knowledge and Human Interests. Trans. Jeremy J. Shapiro. Boston: Beacon Press, 1971

   'The Classical Doctrine of Politics in Relation to Social Philosophy'. Trans. Jeremy J. Shapiro. In Habermas. *Theory and Practice*. Boston: Beacon Press, 1973

   The Theory of Communicative Action. Trans. Thomas McCarthy. Boston: Beacon Press, 1984

   The Philosophical Discourse of Modernity: Twelve Lectures. Cambridge: Polity Press, 1987

Harding, Sandra. *The Science Question in Feminism*. Ithaca, N.Y.: Cornell University Press, 1986

   Whose Science? Whose Knowledge?: Thinking from Women's Lives. Ithaca, N.Y.: Cornell University Press, 1991

Harris, Leonard. 'Review of *The Restructuring of Social and Political Theory*'. *International Philosophical Quarterly*, 19, No. 4 (1979), 485–91

Hegel, G. W. F. *The Phenomenology of Mind*. Trans. J. B. Baillie. New York: Harper and Row, 1967

Heilbroner, Robert L. *Marxism: For and Against*. New York: W. W. Norton & Co., 1980

Held, David. *Introduction to Critical Theory: Horkheimer to Habermas*. Berkeley: University of California Press, 1980

Herz, John. *The Nation-State and the Crisis of World Politics*. New York: David McKay, 1976

Higgott, Richard, ed. *New Directions in International Relations? Australian Perspectives*. Canberra: The Australian National University, 1988

Hoffman, Mark. 'Critical Theory and the Inter-Paradigm Debate'. *Millennium*, 16, No. 2 (1987), 231–49

'Conversations on Critical International Relations Theory'. *Millennium*, 17, No. 1 (1988), 91–95

Hoffmann, Stanley. *Contemporary Theory in International Relations*. Englewood Cliffs, N.J.: Prentice-Hall, 1960

Hollis, Martin, and Steve Smith. *Explaining and Understanding International Relations*. Oxford: Clarendon Press, 1990

Holsti, Kal J. *The Dividing Discipline: Hegemony and Diversity in International Theory*. Boston: Allen & Unwin, 1985

'Mirror, Mirror on the Wall, Which are the Fairest Theories of All?' *International Studies Quarterly*, 33, No. 3, (1989), 255–61

Holsti, Ole. 'The Belief System and National Images: A Case Study'. *Journal of Conflict Resolution*, 6 (1962), 244–52

Horkheimer, Max. 'Die gesellschaftliche Funktion der Philosophie', 'Bemerkungen über Wissenschaft und Krise', and 'Traditionelle und Kritische Theorie'. In Alfred Schmidt, ed. *Kritische Theorie: Eine Dokumentation*. 2 vols. Frankfurt: S. Fischer Verlag, 1968

Critical Theory: Selected Essays. Trans. Matthew J. O'Connell. New York: Continuum, 1989

Jay, Martin. *Marxism and Totality*. Los Angeles: University of California Press, 1984

Kant, Immanuel. *Critique of Pure Reason*. Trans. Norman Kemp Smith. London: Macmillan, 1929

Keohane, Robert O. 'International Institutions: Two Approaches'. *International Studies Quarterly*, 32, No. 4 (1988), 379–96

Keohane, Robert O., ed. *Neorealism and Its Critics*. New York: Columbia University Press, 1986

Klein, Bradley. *Strategic Studies and World Order*. Cambridge: Cambridge University Press, 1994

Knorr, Klaus, and James N. Rosenau, eds. *Contending Approaches to International Politics*. Princeton, N.J.: Princeton University Press, 1969

Kolakowski, Leszek. *The Alienation of Reason: A History of Positivist Thought*. Trans. Norbert Guterman. New York: Doubleday, 1968

Kortian, Garbis. *Métacritique*. Paris: Editions de Minuit, 1979

Krasner, Stephen D., ed. *International Regimes*. Ithaca, N.Y.: Cornell University Press, 1983

Kratochwil, Friedrich. 'Errors have their advantage'. *International Organization*, 38, No. 2 (1984), 305–20

'Regimes, Interpretation and the "Science" of Politics: A Reappraisal'. *Millennium*, 17, No. 2 (1988), 263–84

167

Kratochwil, Friedrich, and John Gerard Ruggie. 'International Organization: A State of the Art on an Art of the State'. *International Organization*, 40, No. 4 (1986), 753–75

Kuhn, Thomas. *The Structure of Scientific Revolutions*. 2nd edn. Chicago: University of Chicago Press, 1970

Lakatos, Imre, and Alan Musgrave, eds. *Criticism and the Growth of Knowledge*. London: Cambridge University Press, 1970

Lapid, Yosef. 'The Third Debate: On the Prospects of International Theory in a Post-Positivist Era'. *International Studies Quarterly*, 33, No. 3 (1989), 235–54

Leonard, Stephen T. *Critical Theory in Political Practice*. Princeton, N.J.: Princeton University Press, 1990

Linklater, Andrew. *Men and Citizens in the Theory of International Relations*. London: Macmillan, 1982

'Realism, Marxism and Critical International Theory'. *Review of International Studies*, 12, No. 4 (1986), 301–12

Beyond Realism and Marxism: Critical Theory and International Relations. New York: St Martin's Press, 1990

Little, Richard, and Steve Smith, eds. *Belief Systems and International Relations*. Oxford: Blackwell, 1988

Lubin, Carol Riegelman, and Anne Winslow. *Social Justice for Women: The International Labour Organizations and Women*. Durham: Duke University Press, 1990

Lukes, Steven. *Moral Conflict and Politics*. Oxford: Clarendon Press, 1991

McCarthy, Thomas A. *The Critical Theory of Jürgen Habermas*. Cambridge, Mass.: MIT Press, 1978

McKinlay, R. D., and R. Little. *Global Problems and World Order*. Madison: University of Wisconsin Press, 1986

Mansbach, Richard W., and Yale H. Ferguson. *The Elusive Quest: Theory and International Politics*. Columbia, S.C.: University of South Carolina Press, 1988

Marcuse, Herbert. *One-Dimensional Man*. Boston: Beacon Press, 1964

Marx, Karl. 'Der Achtzehnte Brumaire des Louis Bonaparte' and 'Thesen über Feuerbach'. In *Karl Marx und Friedrich Engels: Ausgewählte Werke*. Moscow: Progress Publishers, 1981

May, Ernest. *'Lessons' of the Past: The Use and Misuse of History in American Foreign Policy*. New York: Oxford University Press, 1973

May, Ernest, and Richard Neustadt. *Thinking in Time*. New York: Free Press, 1986

Morgenthau, Hans J. 'The Nature and Limits of a Theory of International Relations'. In William T. R. Fox, ed. *Theoretical Aspects of International Relations*. Notre Dame, Ind.: University of Notre Dame Press, 1959

Politics Among Nations: The Struggle for Power and Peace. 6th edn. New York: Knopf, 1985

Naegele, Kaspar D. 'Some Observations on the Scope of Sociological Analysis'. In T. Parsons, M. Shils, and E. Naegele, eds. *Theories of Society:*

Foundations of Modern Sociological Theory, Vol. I. New York: Free Press, 1961

Nardin, Terry, and David R. Mapel, eds. *Traditions of International Ethics.* Cambridge: Cambridge University Press, 1992

Nicholson, Michael. *The Scientific Analysis of Social Behaviour.* London: Frances Pinter, 1983
  Formal Theories in International Relations. Cambridge: Cambridge University Press, 1989
  Rationality and the Analysis of International Conflict. Cambridge: Cambridge University Press, 1992

Onuf, Nicholas G. *World of Our Making: Rules and Rule in Social Theory and International Relations.* Columbia, S.C.: University of South Carolina Press, 1989

Outhwaite, William. *New Philosophies of Social Science: Realism, Hermeneutics and Critical Theory.* Basingstoke: Macmillan, 1987

Oye, Kenneth A., ed. *Cooperation Under Anarchy.* Princeton, N.J.: Princeton University Press, 1985

Peterson, V. Spike, ed. *Gendered States: Feminist (Re)Visions of International Relations Theory.* Boulder: Lynne Rienner, 1992

Popper, Karl. *The Logic of Scientific Discovery.* London: Hutchinson, 1968
  Conjectures and Refutations: The Growth of Scientific Knowledge. 3rd edn. London: Routledge and Kegan Paul, 1969

Rabinow, Paul, and William M. Sullivan, eds. *Interpretive Social Science: A Second Look.* Rev. edn. Berkeley: University of California Press, 1987

Reid, Herbert G., and Ernest J. Yanarella. 'Toward a Critical Theory of Peace Research in the United States: the Search for an 'Intelligible Core''. *Journal of Peace Research*, 13, No. 4 (1976), 315–41

Rengger, N. J. 'Going Critical? A Response to Hoffman'. *Millennium*, 17, No. 1 (1988), 81–9

Rivage-Seul, Marguerite. 'Peace Education: Imagination and the Pedagogy of the Oppressed'. *Harvard Educational Review*, 57, No. 2 (1987), 153–69

Rockmore, Tom, ed. *Lukács Today: Essays in Marxist Philosophy.* Boston: D. Reidel Publishing Company, 1988

Rorty, Richard. *Philosophy and the Mirror of Nature.* Princeton, N.J.: Princeton University Press, 1979
  Consequences of Pragmatism. Brighton: Harvester, 1982

Rosenau, James N. 'Thinking Theory Thoroughly'. In *The Scientific Study of Foreign Policy.* Rev. edn. London: Frances Pinter, 1980
  'Order and Disorder in the Study of World Politics'. In R. Marghoori and B. Ramberg, eds. *Globalism Versus Realism: International Relations Third Debate.* Boulder: Westview, 1982

Rosenau, Pauline. 'Once Again Into the Fray: International Relations Confronts the Humanities'. *Millennium*, 19, No. 1 (1990), 83–110

Runyan, Anne Sisson, and V. Spike Peterson. 'The Radical Future of Realism: Feminist Subversions of IR Theory'. *Alternatives*, 16, No. 1 (1991), 67–106

Bibliography

Sabia, Daniel R., Jr, and Jerald T. Wallulis, eds. *Changing Social Science: Critical Theory and Other Critical Perspectives*. Albany: State University of New York Press, 1983

Sandler, Bernice R. 'The Classroom Climate: Chilly for Women?' In A. Deneef, C. Goodwin, and E. McCrate, eds. *The Academic's Handbook*. London: Duke University Press, 1988

Schell, Jonathan. *The Fate of the Earth*. New York: Alfred A. Knopf, 1982

Seidman, Steven, ed. *Jürgen Habermas on Society and Politics: A Reader*. Boston: Beacon Press, 1989

Singer, J. David. 'The Level-of-Analysis Problem in International Relations'. In K. Knorr and S. Verba, eds. *The International System: Theoretical Essays*. Princeton, N.J.: Princeton University Press, 1961

'The Responsibilities of Competence in the Global Village'. *International Studies Quarterly*, 29, No. 3 (1985), 245–305

Sjolander, Claire, and Wayne Cox, eds. *Beyond Positivism: Critical Reflections on International Relations*. Boulder: Lynne Rienner, 1994

Smith, Steve. 'Paradigm Dominance in International Relations: The Development of International Relations as a Social Science'. *Millennium*, 16, No. 2 (1987), 189–206

'The Forty Years' Detour: The Resurgence of Normative Theory in International Relations'. *Millennium*, 21, No. 3 (1992), 489–506

Smith, Steve, ed. *International Relations: British and American Perspectives*. Oxford: Blackwell, 1985

Sullivan, Michael P. *International Relations: Theories and Evidence*. Englewood Cliffs, N.J.: Prentice-Hall, 1976

Suppe, Frederich. *The Structure of Scientific Theories*. 2nd edn. Urbana: University of Illinois Press, 1977

Sylvester, Christine. *Feminist Theory and International Relations in a Postmodern Era*. Cambridge: Cambridge University Press, 1994

Taylor, Charles. *Hegel and Modern Society*. Cambridge: Cambridge University Press, 1979

Philosophy and the Human Sciences. Cambridge: Cambridge University Press, 1985

'Interpretation and the Sciences of Man'. In Paul Rabinow and William M. Sullivan, eds. *Interpretive Social Science: A Second Look*. Rev. edn. Berkeley: University of California Press, 1987

Thom, Betsy. 'Women in International Organizations: Room at the Top: The Situation in Some United Nations Organizations'. In C. F. Epstein and R. L. Coser, eds. *Access to Power: Cross-National Studies of Women and Elites*. London: George Allen & Unwin, 1981

Thompson, John B. *Critical Hermeneutics: A Study in the Thought of Paul Ricoeur and Jürgen Habermas*. Cambridge: Cambridge University Press, 1981

'The Theory of Structuration'. In David Held and John B. Thompson, eds. *Social Theory of Modern Societies: Anthony Giddens and His Critics*. Cambridge: Cambridge University Press, 1989

Vasquez, John. *The Power of Power Politics: A Critique*. New Brunswick, N.J.: Rutgers University Press, 1983

Vico, Giambattista. *The New Science of Giambattista Vico* (1744). Trans. Thomas Goddard Bergin and Max Harold Fisch. Ithaca, N.Y.: Cornell University Press, 1984

Viotti, Paul R., and Mark V. Kauppi, eds. *International Relations Theory: Realism, Pluralism, Globalism*. New York: Macmillan, 1987

Walker, R. B. J. *One World, Many Worlds: Struggles for a Just World Peace*. Boulder: Lynne Rienner, 1988

'History and Structure in the Theory of International Studies'. *Millennium*, 18, No. 2 (1989), 163–83

Inside/Outside: International Relations as Political Theory. Cambridge: Cambridge University Press, 1993

Waltz, Kenneth. *Man, The State, and War: A Theoretical Analysis*. New York: Columbia University Press, 1959

Theory of International Politics. New York: Random House, 1979

Warnke, Georgia. *Gadamer: Hermeneutics, Tradition, and Reason*. Stanford, Calif.: Stanford University Press, 1987

Justice and Interpretation. Cambridge: Polity Press, 1992

Warren, Scott. *The Emergence of Dialectical Theory: Philosophy and Political Inquiry*. Chicago: University of Chicago Press, 1984

Wendt, Alexander. 'The Agent–Structure Problem in International Relations Theory'. *International Organization*, 41, No. 3 (1987), 335–70

West, Cornel. *The American Evasion of Philosophy*. Madison: The University of Wisconsin Press, 1989

Whitworth, Sandra. 'Gender in the Inter-Paradigm Debate'. *Millennium*, 18, No. 2 (1989), 265–72

Feminism and International Relations. London: Macmillan, 1994

Review of Christine Sylvester, *Feminist Theory and International Relations in a Postmodern Era*. In *Canadian Journal of Political Science*, 28, No. 1 (1995), 177–78

Wight, Martin. 'Why is There No International Theory?' In Herbert Butterfield and Martin Wight, eds. *Diplomatic Investigations: Essays in the Theory of International Politics*. London: George Allen & Unwin, 1966

Williams, Michael C. 'Rousseau, Realism and Realpolitik'. *Millennium*, 18, No. 2 (1989), 188–204

Young, Oran R. *International Cooperation: Building Regimes for Natural Resources and the Environment*. Ithaca, N.Y.: Cornell University Press, 1989

Zalewski, Marysia. 'Feminist Theory and International Relations'. In Mike Bowker and Robin Brown, eds. *From Cold War to Collapse: Theory and World Politics in the 1980s*. Cambridge: Cambridge University Press, 1993.

Index

CAMBRIDGE STUDIES IN INTERNATIONAL RELATIONS